Mozambique

Rising from the Ashes

JENNY MATTHEWS/OXFAM

Contents

Foreword 3
The first states 4
Five centuries of exploitation 5
The long struggle for independence 8
From independence to civil war 10
A nation in flames 12
The quest for peace 15
The challenge of demobilisation 17
Defence systems down 19
Landmines: a bitter harvest 20
Creating a nation 23
Rebuilding broken lives 26
The dwindling of vast lands 29
Assets of the earth and sea 33
Roads to prosperity 39
The economy: painful choices 42
At the end of the rivers 45
Education: hungry minds 49
Health: the jaded jewel 53
A mother's right 59
The challenge of democracy 61
Facts and figures 62
Further reading and sources 63
Oxfam in Mozambique 64

Oxfam UK and Ireland   **Rachel Waterhouse**

1

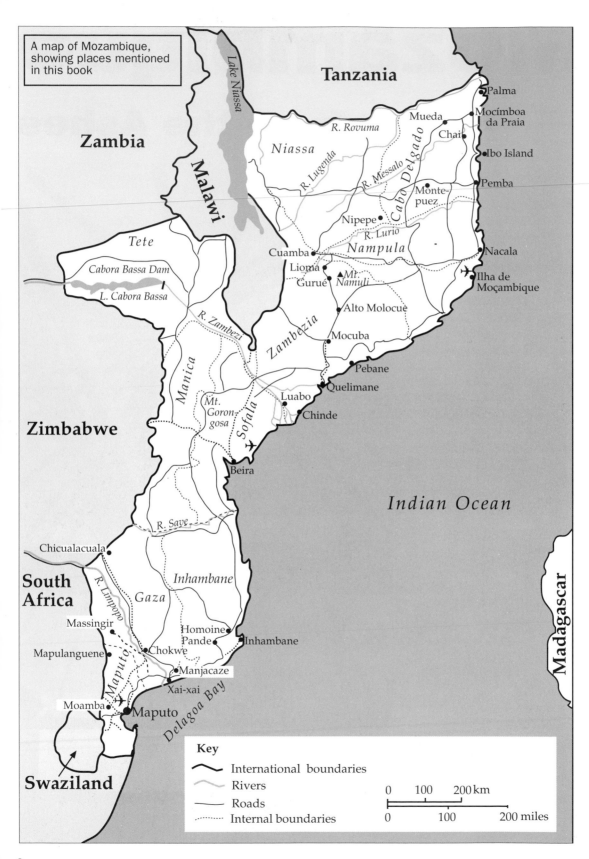

A map of Mozambique, showing places mentioned in this book

Tanzania

Zambia

Malawi

Lake Niassa

Niassa

R. Rovuma

R. Lugenda

R. Messalo

Cabo Delgado

Palma

Mocímboa da Praia

Mueda

Chai

Ibo Island

Monte-puez

Pemba

Nipepe

R. Lurio

Nampula

Cuamba

Lioma

Gurué

▲Mt. Namuli

Alto Molocuè

Nacala

Ilha de Moçambique

Tete

Cabora Bassa Dam

L. Cabora Bassa

R. Zambezi

Manica

Zambezia

Mocuba

Pebane

Quelimane

Sofala

Mt. Goron-gosa

Luabo

Chinde

Beira

Zimbabwe

Indian Ocean

R. Save

Chicualacuala

South Africa

Inhambane

Gaza

R. Limpopo

Massingir

Mapulanguene

Homoine

Pande

Chokwe

Inhambane

Manjacaze

Xai-xai

Moamba

Maputo

Delagoa Bay

Madagascar

Swaziland

Key

━━━ International boundaries

〰 Rivers

─── Roads

⋯⋯ Internal boundaries

0   100   200 km

0   100   200 miles

2

Foreword

Mozambican society, its history and its culture have been forged in the fire of international politics. The flames were kindled 500 years ago, when the first European adventurers arrived to trade in gold, ivory, and slaves. In modern times Mozambique smouldered through a series of liberation struggles, fuelled by weapons supplied by the superpowers. Then came the ultimate conflagration, ignited by sparks from the apartheid regime in neighbouring South Africa: 16 years of civil war, one of the most brutal conflicts ever waged in Africa.

In recent history, Mozambique stands out as one of the rare places where United Nations peace-keeping forces have met with success. Following a Peace Accord in 1992, the UN mission ONUMOZ guided Mozambique's transition from violent conflict to nominal peace and democracy.

The peace process officially ended when the nation held its first ever multi-party, democratic elections in October 1994. Thereupon, ONUMOZ packed up and left. After a brief exposure in the glare of international attention, Mozambique disappeared from the headlines. Yet for its 17 million people another struggle was just beginning: to repair the shattered fabric of their lives, and complete the task of forging a truly Mozambican nation.

Repairing the Beira railway line

The first states

The modern boundaries of Mozambique were not defined until the late nineteenth century. For centuries before that, kings and warlords rose and fell, populations settled and migrated, and frontiers between competing societies constantly shifted.

The first organised state to control part of the territory now called Mozambique was thirteenth-century Zimbabwe, whose rulers lived in stone-walled citadels. Two hundred years later this civilisation declined, giving way to the Muenemutapa Empire, which at its height in the sixteenth century was probably the largest and most powerful state of Central and Southern Africa, extending from the Kalahari Desert to the Indian Ocean.

To the north of the Muenemutapa, the powerful Maravi kingdoms straddled today's Malawi and northern Mozambique. To the south lived the Tonga peoples, governed by chiefly dynasties.

In the land now known a Mozambique, farmers grew sorghum and millet. on the coast, people fished; in the south, they bred cattle. The ruling aristocracies controlled taxes and international trade. The Muenemutapa chiefs levied a tax on agriculture and controlled the production of many gold mines, where thousands of their subjects were forced to labour and sweat. They also controlled the gold trade with Swahili-speaking Arab merchants settling on the coast. Maravi leaders, meanwhile, traded in ivory. In exchange, they received imported cloth from India, Persian pottery, Venetian beads, and later, firearms.

Arab traders from the Persian Gulf had settled on Mozambique's northern coast as early as the ninth century, mingling with indigenous peoples to create a rich and varied coastal culture. New languages evolved, blending Arabic and Swahili with local tongues; Islamic religion mingled with African beliefs in magic and spiritual powers. Muslim sultans and sheiks ran a flourishing import–export business from East Africa to the Indies.

Maintaining their own settlements on the shores of the Indian Ocean, the Swahili-Arab traders established complex commercial networks with African chiefs of the interior — a model which Portuguese settlers were later to adopt.

Traditional Mapiko masks, used in ceremonies of the Makonde people in Cabo Delgado
JENNY MATTHEWS/OXFAM

Five centuries of exploitation

Gold, ivory — and slavery

When the first Portuguese settlers reached northern Mozambique, at the turn of the fifteenth century, their aim was not to create a unified state — merely to capture the lucrative gold trade from the Swahili-Arab merchants. This they eventually did; but from the end of the seventeenth century the trade in gold was largely replaced by ivory exports to the East — a trade which was itself superseded from the 1760s by a roaring slave trade to the French colonies, Brazil, Cuba, and northern America.

Conniving with local chiefs and Swahili merchants, the Portuguese probably sold at least one million Mozambicans into slavery before the trade finally died out at the turn of the nineteenth century. Mozambique was thus robbed of untold human potential, while whole communities were driven into hiding in the most isolated and hostile recesses of their country.

Throughout the first 400 years of colonial penetration, the Portuguese invaders brought virtually no new technology to Mozambique. Their one-way process of extracting resources had already laid the foundations for long-term under-development.

The colonists tighten their grip

Until the nineteenth century, Portuguese rule in Mozambique was limited to a few coastal settlements and a tenuous hold on the lush but malaria-infested Zambezi Valley, settled by Portuguese *prazeiros* (land-holders) who inter-married with Africans, ran their own slave-armies, and had only dubious allegiance to the Portuguese crown. Commerce was largely in the hands of Indian merchants, who had established a vast trading network in the north and centre of the country.

It was only at the end of the century, when competition intensified between the European colonial powers in the so-called 'Scramble for Africa', that Portugal sought to extend administrative control throughout Mozambique. Its main competitor was Britain, though Afrikaners and Germans were also jostling for territory.

The modern boundaries of Mozambique were eventually agreed in 1891, by political bargaining between Portugal — claiming historic right to the territory — and Britain — keen to extend its neighbouring colony of Southern Rhodesia and gain access to Mozambique's minerals and ports.

Portugal's early attempts to 'pacify' Mozambique met with fierce African resistance. In the south the Portuguese faced the great Gaza kingdom, established by Nguni warriors early in the century. At its height, the Gaza kingdom ran from south of the Limpopo River as far as the Zambezi. The Nguni ruler, Gungunhana, played off one colonial power against the

A monument in Maputo Fort depicts the capture of the Emperor of Gaza by Portuguese invaders
JENNY MATTHEWS/OXFAM

other, but his 20,000-man army, armed by the British, was finally shot down by superior Portuguese fire-power in 1895, and Gungunhana was forced into exile.

The privatisation of the State

The Portuguese conquered the Zambezi Valley in 1902, and the northern Macua and Yao ten years later. But the colonial state of the twentieth century failed to unite the national territory which the Portuguese called Mozambique. The early government was notoriously weak. Unable to run things itself, it contracted out the 'pacification', administration, and development of most of the colony to private companies, leaving the southern quarter of the state as a labour reserve for the gold mines of South Africa.

From 1891 to 1941, control of central Mozambique was given to the Mozambique Company, formed with British and French capital and empowered to raise taxes, grant mineral and land concessions, and issue currency and postage stamps. A similar Charter granted 100,000 square miles of land north of the Lurio River to the Nyassa Company, owned by British and French interests. The Zambezi Valley was divided among various smaller concerns, the largest of which was the British Sena Sugar Estates.

These companies raised their main income through taxation and forced labour from the local population. The Portuguese exploited the traditional institution of land chiefs, either by co-opting them or by replacing them with *regulos* (chiefs) of their own choosing. Paid by the State, the *regulos* were responsible for collecting taxes, maintaining order, and recruiting workers for the hated *chibalo* system of forced labour. Until as late as 1961, Mozambicans were press-ganged to work on colonial plantations, to build roads and railways, or perform any other task required by the Portuguese.

The colonial government made virtually no welfare provision for the African peoples. Education was entrusted to the Catholic Church. Scarce places, high fees, and age restrictions meant that by 1960 only one per cent of Mozambican children were in secondary school. Medical care was almost exclusively reserved to the cities, though 94 per cent of the African population lived in the countryside.

Exporting people

In 1926 a coup in Portugal brought the fascist dictator Antonio Salazar to power. Salazar took back control of Mozambique from the charter companies and formalised the 'Indigenous Peoples' Rule', whereby African and mixed-race people were divided into two groups. The tiny minority who could read and write Portuguese, rejected traditional customs, and had professional employment were considered honorary Portuguese or 'assimilated' citizens in the eyes of the law. The rest had no legal rights, were obliged to carry identity cards, and had to fulfil forced-labour requirements. By the eve of national independence in 1975, only one per cent of the African population had been 'assimilated'.

With the end of the slave trade and the declining commercial importance of the north, in 1902 the Portuguese moved their original capital from Ilha de Mocambique, off the northern coast, to Delagoa Bay in the far south. The new capital city of Lourenço Marques (renamed Maputo after national Independence) became a major international port; much of the city's infrastructure, including its first modern wharf, was financed by British capital.

While the north was neglected and declined, the economy of southern Mozambique became intrinsically linked with the more powerful economy of neighbouring South Africa, through trading networks and the export of Mozambican labour to the South African gold mines. Through agreement with South Africa in 1901, the colonial government received a recruitment tax on each Mozambican worker exported and then took a commission amounting to half of the workers' wages, paid in gold.

In the early 1900s, in any one year Mozambique was exporting over 80,000 mine workers to South Africa, while revenue from South African trade through Lourenço Marques port accounted for one third of the colonial state's income. In central Mozambique, Africans either worked on colonial farms or were exported to Southern Rhodesia (now Zimbabwe). In some parts of the country, up to half of the male population was absent at any one time, leaving women and children to do most of the agricultural work at home, as well as *chibalo* for the colonials.

While Portugal used Mozambique to supply raw materials for its own industry (especially cotton for textiles), low prices and prohibitive laws stifled the development of manufacturing industry in the colony. Thus Mozambique became a crucial market for exports from Portugal, known then as the 'poor man of Europe'.

Throughout this period, hundreds of thousands of Mozambicans fled from their country to British-run territories over the border (where colonial rule was a little less oppressive), to avoid *chibalo* and the prevailing violence of the Portuguese regime.

Colonial architecture: Maputo railway station
JENNY MATTHEWS/OXFAM

Ressano Garcia station: migrant workers returning to Mozambique from South Africa
JULIAN QUAN/OXFAM

The long struggle for independence

Following the great battles which finally put an end to the independent African kingdoms of Mozambique at the turn of the nineteenth century, for several decades revolts against colonial rule were local and sporadic. African opposition was quickly suppressed by the government authorities, its secret police (PIDE), armed police force, and the military.

In the mid-1960s, the tide turned. To Mozambicans, the Mueda massacre of 1960 marks the symbolic prelude to a new phase in organised resistance. Already by that year, growing nationalism in Africa had inspired the birth of several opposition groups, formed by Mozambicans living or working abroad in Southern Rhodesia, Malawi, and the dockyards and plantations of Kenya and Tanzania.

MANU (Mozambican-Makonde Union) was the first to start mobilising support within Mozambique, starting among Makonde people in the mountainous forests of Cabo Delgado Province. Working secretly through a network of agricultural co-operatives, MANU gained popularity. In June 1960, its supporters helped to stage a peaceful demonstration outside the Portuguese administrator's office in Mueda. The Governor responded with arrests; the crowd protested, and he ordered his troops to open fire. Some 600 peaceful demonstrators died in the slaughter. Immediately the colonial State banned all African organisations of more than 30 people.

In 1962, the President of independent Tanzania, Julius Nyerere, invited MANU and two other groups, UDENAMO and UNAMI, to set up their headquarters in the Tanzanian capital of Dar Es Salaam, encouraging them to join forces. They fused to form the Liberation Front of Mozambique, FRELIMO, in June 1962.

FRELIMO is formed

Educated in Portugal, South Africa, and the USA, Eduardo Mondlane, FRELIMO's first president, was also the first Mozambican to achieve a doctor's degree. He left his post at the United Nations to lead a revolution.

FRELIMO launched its ten-year guerrilla struggle against colonial rule in September 1964. With a rear base in Tanzania and strong Makonde support, the guerrillas met quick success in the north. Driving out the Portuguese, FRELIMO re-organised African villagers in what it named the 'liberated zones'. Defining class, not race, as the main cause of oppression in Mozambique, FRELIMO set up schools, literacy classes, shops, and health clinics in the rural areas under its control.

A mural in Chai, Cabo Delgado, commemorating the liberation struggle
JENNY MATTHEWS/OXFAM

President Samora Machel, commemorated in the Museum of the Revolution

FRELIMO's initial success was marred by deep internal divisions, which would re-emerge later to weaken the party. While Eduardo Mondlane and his southern intellectual supporters favoured a full-blown social revolution to change class relations, many other members, especially northerners, were traditionalists who merely wanted to oust the Portuguese. Defectors from FRELIMO were suspected of collaborating with the secret police to murder Eduardo Mondlane by means of a parcel bomb.

Samora Machel takes over

Mondlane's murder was followed by a leadership struggle between northerners and southerners. FRELIMO Commander Samora Machel, born in southern Gaza Province like Mondlane, was eventually appointed its president in 1970. Internal differences were forthwith suppressed in the overwhelming effort to win the war.

While other European states like Britain and France were decolonising, Portugal clung to colonial rule. It received continued Western support, including military aid from the USA. FRELIMO, by contrast, became increasingly hostile to the West and closer to China and the Soviet Union, the only countries willing to give it military support.

As FRELIMO military success began to spread from northern to central Mozambique, in 1974 an army coup in Portugal ousted Salazar's hand-picked successor, Marcello Caetano, from power. The coup was provoked by the heavy cost of fighting losing battles in all of Portugal's African colonies. It brought sudden victory for Mozambique's freedom fighters.

An agreement with Portugal's new rulers handed State power to FRELIMO, without a democratic mandate from the Mozambican peoples. FRELIMO, indeed, immediately suppressed all other political activity, arresting several hundred opposition-party members in its campaign against 'the enemy within', including the 'bourgeois saboteurs' and people regarded as collaborators with the colonial regime. Some opposition leaders were later executed.

Mozambicans were to wait another 20 years before they were able to vote in pluralist elections.

From independence to civil war

National Independence was declared in 1975, and in response virtually all the Portuguese colonials and many of the Asian traders left Mozambique in a mass exodus.

FRELIMO inherited a fragmented nation, governed by colonial laws and a weak administrative machinery. Some 98 per cent of its African population were illiterate. The fleeing Portuguese took with them whatever goods and capital they could, plus all their technical and managerial skills. What they could not carry — tractors, buildings, cattle — they destroyed. Commercial production and rural and urban trade collapsed in their wake.

Catapulted to power from a guerrilla bush war, FRELIMO was faced with economic chaos and continued hostility from some Western governments. The communist world offered military support, and limited material aid to help FRELIMO realise its ambitious goals of redistributing wealth to the poor,

extending health and education services, and propelling Mozambique into rapid growth and development.

In its eagerness to do all these things, FRELIMO dropped its self-definition as a 'party of the masses' in 1977, renaming itself a vanguard party, with the self-appointed task of leading the masses. It adopted Marxism-Leninism as its official doctrine. Land, health care, and education were nationalised, and many buildings were appropriated by the State. The government stepped in to run abandoned farms, companies, and shops.

Before long, Mozambique won international praise for its success in extending health care and increasing literacy, while production seemed to be up and running again. Primary-school enrolment doubled in the first six years of FRELIMO rule, and the annual secondary-school intake increased from 20,000 to 135,000. By 1979, health workers, often tramping barefoot through the countryside to vaccinate people against smallpox, tetanus, and measles, had reached some 90 per cent of the population. Infant mortality had fallen by 20 per cent.

The honeymoon, however, was short. FRELIMO had little experience of government and very few resources. Its agricultural policy was a failure. Its ten-year programme for rapid, centrally planned and heavily capitalised development proved to be a fantasy. Economic problems were compounded by drought and growing insecurity in the countryside.

Moreover, Mozambique had gained independence in the tense years of the mid-1970s, when the superpowers of East and West were perilously engaged in the Cold War. The battle for independence raged on in southern Africa, and in

Commercial production collapsed after the abrupt departure of Portuguese colonists
KEITH BERNSTEIN/OXFAM

Primary-school enrolment doubled in the first six years of Independence

neighbouring South Africa the apparatus of apartheid was firmly in place. As a champion of the nationalist cause, the new FRELIMO government gave its support to fighters for a free Zimbabwe in Southern Rhodesia and to the African National Congress, struggling to end apartheid in South Africa. Mozambique was punished with military retribution and heavily damaging trade sanctions, inflicted by hostile neighbouring governments.

By the mid-1980s, famine was widespread, thousands of people were starving, and thousands more were fleeing from their homes before a rapidly spreading civil conflict.

The end of the Machel era

Samora Machel was Mozambique's charismatic first President, and self-styled 'father' of the nation. Despite his communist label, he never cut ties with the West, and by the mid-1980s he was already pushing his government towards more liberal policies.

The mystery of his sudden death in a plane crash over South Africa on 19 October 1986 remains unsolved. Many Mozambicans leapt to the conclusion that

he had been assassinated by agents of South Africa's apartheid government. But political rumour suggests that southern-born Machel could have been the victim of divisions in his own party, not only over policy, but over the old regional/ethnic differences.

Its economy in a shambles, in 1987 Mozambique eventually entered a classic agreement with Western financiers: in return for more credit, FRELIMO would adopt a 'structural adjustment programme' aimed at economic liberalisation.

Following the economic initiative through to its political conclusion, Machel's successor Joaquim Chissano oversaw FRELIMO's official transformation from a Marxist-Leninist party to a 'social democratic' identity in 1989. In 1990 FRELIMO itself introduced a new national constitution, removing the State's monopoly on many areas of life, while enshrining respect for freedom of the individual, human rights, property rights, and multi-party democracy.

But economic prosperity and political democracy would be impossible to realise in the context of the civil war now raging in the countryside.

A nation in flames

By the time FRELIMO began to liberalise its policies in the mid-1980s, it had already earned many enemies at home. The 'party of workers and peasants' had challenged the colonial elite for power, but replaced it with an elite of young party cadres. It conducted an intolerant campaign against all authorities linked to the colonial state, including the *regulos*, religious leaders, and *curandeiros* (herbalists and spirit mediums) who had guided the traditional order and moral life of Mozambican communities. Polygamists were banned from the party, and traditional leaders were ostracised.

Despite its good intentions, FRELIMO's radical reforms offended traditional values and stirred intense resentment among many of the new outcasts. The situation was dangerously combustible — but the spark that lit the tinder was thrown in from the outside.

RENAMO

The rebel group RENAMO (Mozambican National Resistance) was created by Southern Rhodesia's security forces, in retaliation for FRELIMO's support for ZANLA guerrillas fighting for an independent Zimbabwe. By 1977 the group had a trickle of Mozambican recruits, including a former FRELIMO commander, Andre Matsangaissa, who escaped from Mozambique after a conviction for theft and became RENAMO's first president.

At first, under the wing of the Rhodesian military, the rebels attacked FRELIMO and ZANLA bases inside Mozambique. In practice, this meant setting villages aflame, destroying clinics, shops, and railways, and vandalising commerce.

When Zimbabwe gained independence in 1980, RENAMO seemed to be finished — until the South African military

(SADF) decided to adopt it. For the next few years, RENAMO was funded, trained, and equipped by South Africa's apartheid rulers, as part of its regional policy of 'destabilisation'. This aimed to weaken the socialist governments which were gradually replacing colonial regimes throughout southern Africa and counter any support they might give to opponents of apartheid rule.

Until 1989, RENAMO's training and intelligence gathering was based at Phalaborwa in South Africa. Roads, railways, power plants, and other economic installations in Mozambique were prime targets, but so were all social symbols of FRELIMO: State-run schools, health centres, and local administrations, and the people who staffed them.

Captured RENAMO documents and its own members testified that RENAMO saw civilians as legitimate targets. In the early years, its tactics included slicing off the noses, ears, and sexual organs of victims. Civilian accounts tell of RENAMO forcing people to watch their relatives murdered; of boys forced to kill parents; girls raped; children boiled alive.

RENAMO's foreign backers promoted its external image as an anti-communist liberation movement. In the Cold War context, this helped it to win backing from right-wing and religious groups in the West. The pro-Western president of Malawi, Hastings Banda, allowed RENAMO to use his country as a rear base. Apparently he was encouraged by his own ambitions to gain control of part of northern Mozambique, reviving the Maravi domain of the seventeenth century. Kenya, a long-time refuge for anti-FRELIMO Mozambicans, and the Comoros Isles were also used as supply routes.

From puppets to warlords

Though the creation of foreigners, RENAMO soon developed a life of its own, feeding on the resentment of people whom FRELIMO had deposed or ostracised. Eventually its brutality alienated many people who initially were sympathetic, but by this time RENAMO had rooted itself in other ways.

In 1984, Mozambique and South Africa signed the Nkomati friendship accord. South Africa pledged to end its support for RENAMO, in return for Mozambique's promise not to allow the ANC any military bases on its soil. South Africa transferred RENAMO headquarters to the deep forests of the Gorongosa mountains in central Mozambique, where it stockpiled weapons and supplies. Covert South African support continued, but from then on RENAMO was more dependent on its own resources.

The epicentre of the war was central Mozambique, where RENAMO fought its hardest battles. Feeding on anti-FRELIMO and anti-southern resentment, it became rooted in the Ndau ethnic group of Matsangaissa and his successor after his death, Afonso Dhlakama. Recruitment was generally done on the crude and ancient basis of forcing captured men and boys to join up, on pain of torture or death if they tried to escape.

In central Mozambique, RENAMO's operations came to resemble those of the ancient warlords, exacting tribute from local communities in return for giving them 'protection'. Increasingly, RENAMO survived on tributes and by raiding and looting target populations.

In zones that fell under its control, RENAMO left local administration in the hands of the former *regulos*, or appointed new ones. From its base in the wildlife reserve of Gorongosa, it made money from illegal ivory trading. Yet it occupied no towns, and by the end of the war controlled no significant economic enterprise. Rudimentary health care and education in RENAMO areas were carried out by workers trained under FRELIMO or by captured FRELIMO supporters.

As RENAMO spread into northern Mozambique, its anti-government stance won some sympathy among the Muslim coastal populations. In the FRELIMO-dominated south, however, it found little acceptance. Here, rather than setting up large bases, it would go on raids of destruction. The worst massacres of the war took place in the south.

For years, the government refused to admit that civil war was really going on. The State-controlled press spoke only of 'armed bandit' activity. On the ground, FRELIMO retaliated strongly, sometimes with great brutality, against any communities suspected of supporting the guerrilla insurgents.

Zambezia Province, 1990: a mother and child, seeking safety from RENAMO attacks, at a camp for displaced people in Alto Molocue

SARAH ERRINGTON/OXFAM

Nothing left to fight for

Civil war reached its height in 1986/87. Two years later it was obvious that no military victory was possible, in this conflict fought by ragged and often bootless soldiers. Government forces were not strong enough to wipe out the rebels; RENAMO was not strong enough to force the government out of power. When widespread drought struck Mozambique in 1990/92, the crops withered and the land cracked, and eventually there was nothing left to fight over, not even food.

External support for the war and its supposed ideological differences were also disappearing fast. The end of the Cold War meant an end of East European support for FRELIMO, which had already chosen the road to liberalisation. As the government moved closer to the West, RENAMO found it harder to win support on the basis of being anti-communist. In 1988, the rebel movement was discredited by Robert Gersony's report to the US State Department, holding RENAMO responsible for some 100,000 deaths (mainly of civilians). The gradual end of apartheid in South Africa and democratic changes in Malawi were perhaps the death knell of RENAMO's military chances.

Foreign Minister Joaquim Chissano succeeded Machel as President in 1987. With the help first of the Zimbabwe and Kenya governments and then of Italy and the Catholic Church, a long search for peace began. Direct peace talks started in 1990 and were concluded on 4 October 1992 with a Peace Accord signed in Rome.

The toll of war was tremendous. According to UN estimates, close to one million lives were lost through war, hunger and diseases. Nearly two million refugees fled to neighbouring countries, while an estimated four million people were internally displaced (from a total population of 17 million). Mozambican Finance Ministry calculations put the cost of 'damage and lost development' at $15 billion. Schools and health posts across the country lay burned out or abandoned, industry was in ruins, domestic transport at a standstill. By 1994, over two million Mozambicans still depended on international food aid. Mozambique was among the poorest nations in the world, with an average annual income per head of only $88.00, and two thirds of its population living in 'absolute poverty', according to the World Bank. It was the most indebted country in the world (relative to income), and the most aid-dependent.

One of countless bridges destroyed during the civil war

DANIEL MULLINS/OXFAM

The quest for peace

Immediately after signing the Rome Peace Accord, the government and RENAMO called on the United Nations for help with its implementation. Under the guidance of Aldo Ajello, an Italian politician turned UN diplomat, the United Nations Operation in Mozambique (ONUMOZ) was to prove one of its most successful ventures since the end of the Cold War.

Mozambique's two-year transition from civil war to peace was funded by the international community, which paid some one million US dollars a day for UN supervision of the peace process. The UN's role was principally one of mediation and monitoring. It had to oversee the dismantling of the rival government and guerrilla armies, seek out undeclared weapons and clear landmines, oversee the formation of a new national army (combining former government and RENAMO forces), and monitor the nation's first-ever multi-party elections, planned as the culmination of Mozambique's transition to peace.

UN agencies also assumed responsibility for delivering food aid to the destitute, assisting the return of refugees from abroad, and aiding the resettlement of returning refugees, displaced people, and demobilised soldiers. The United Nations Humanitarian Assistance Committee, UNOHAC, was set up to co-ordinate the work of the UN and bilateral and non-governmental organisations (NGOs) in these areas.

The lessons of Angola and Somalia

ONUMOZ went into action against the background of two recent disasters in UN peace-keeping. Just as Mozambique signed a Peace Accord, its 'twin' ex-Portuguese colony of Angola was plunging back into civil war, following

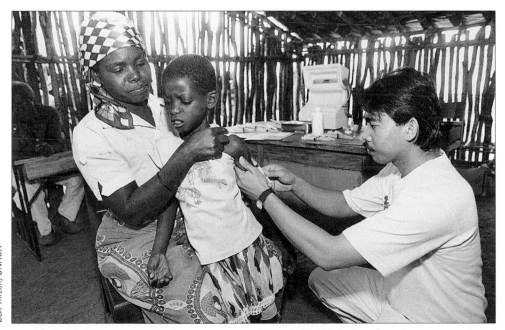

UNHCR transit camp at Changara, Tete Province: vaccinations for children returning to Mozambique after the civil war

the failure of a UN-monitored peace process that was meant to end the conflict between Angola's government and UNITA rebels. The UN was widely criticised for sending a merely token force of some 800 peace-keepers to Angola, and for allowing elections to take place while both sides still controlled separate armies.

To avoid a similar failure, the UN agreed to send Mozambique a far larger force of up to 7,000 troops, plus civilian staff, while Aldo Ajello insisted: no elections before full demobilisation of Mozambique's rival armies.

On the other hand, ONUMOZ deliberately avoided the interventionist 'peace-making' role that led the UN into a lethal farce in Somalia, where it came into direct conflict with the Somali militia. UN troops in Mozambique had no mandate,

and fortunately no call, to intervene in any armed conflict. Making peace was left in the hands of Mozambicans. As Ajello said at the end of his mission, it was thanks above all to Mozambicans' collective will for peace that peace was achieved.

The end at last

Inevitably there were problems. The UN took almost ten months to deploy its 6,500 peace-keeping troops from 21 different countries. RENAMO lacked trained personnel to sit on the official peace-keeping commissions. But one sign of progress was the agreement of RENAMO President, Afonso Dhlakama, to leave his wartime base in Gorongosa and move into a luxury mansion in Maputo. In December 1993, troops from the two rival armies began to assemble into separate camps.

Peace held, tenuously. Using the tactics of brinkmanship and threats of return to war, RENAMO tried to squeeze a deal from FRELIMO on sharing power, regardless of the results in coming elections. Hawks within the government's military establishment meanwhile fought hard to maintain their own power. Both sides missed successive deadlines to start demobilising troops.

Eventually there were widespread mutinies in the assembly camps, where idle and frustrated soldiers paradoxically made a violent thrust for peace. Tired of war and fed up with empty promises, disillusioned soldiers demanded to go home. Lives were lost in their protests.

Demobilisation finally began and in August 1994 the rival forces were both formally abolished. Their place was taken by the joint new Armed Defence Forces of Mozambique (FADM). ONUMOZ allowed the election campaign to begin. It was relatively free of intimidation, and in October 1994 there was a massive popular turn-out, when virtually all Mozambicans voted for one thing: peace.

Neither ONUMOZ nor the peace process had been flawless, but overall the transition from civil war and a one-party system was remarkably successful.

Demobilisation of the rival armies was spurred on by the demands of war-weary soldiers

JENNY MATTHEWS/OXFAM

The challenge of demobilisation

The war was over, but the advent of peace created new problems. For example: how can a shattered economy absorb thousands of frustrated and unskilled ex-soldiers?

Demobilisation of the rival armies began in March 1994. By the end of the UN mandate, some 75,000 troops from both sides had been discharged. UNICEF and the Red Cross rescued hundreds of child soldiers from RENAMO bases.

Promises, promises

Most of the rag-tag recruits were eager to go home. The government promised pay awards to all soldiers, from both sides. RENAMO was promising political victory and a post-elections share of the power to its troops. Yet, as the men languished for months on end in over-crowded and ill-equipped assembly camps, the promises went sour, and the ex-fighters began to fear for their own future.

On the government's side, many soldiers had been conscripted into the army aged 18, or younger, often before they had finished their studies. Officially, national service was meant to last two years, but countless conscripts found themselves stuck in the army for over a decade. Despite its hardships, the army provided pay, food, lodging, and uniforms. Notoriously it also provided the cover for officers and men to carry out illicit operations. Near the end of the war, as the conflict degenerated into skirmishes and robberies, a common popular dictum described some government troops as 'FRELIMO by day, RENAMO by night' (when they would join in the looting).

In the case of RENAMO, captured men and boys had been initiated into the guerrilla ranks, often through occult ceremonies or ritual killings. From there,

as one former captive put it, 'there was no deadline for service'.

Thousands of fighters who got their marching orders in 1994 now faced the challenge of economic survival without any other professional skills, or sometimes even literacy skills. They flooded on to a job market offering very few places in formal employment. In compensation, the government promised all ex-soldiers six months' demobilisation pay, based on former government salaries; but, with the average soldier's monthly pay amounting to a mere US$6.00, it was a paltry deal.

Buying time for elections

Soldiers and ex-soldiers began to stage violent protests in many parts of the country. They blocked roads, took hostages, threatened UN personnel, and even beat up their own officers.

Under the Peace Accord, a tripartite Re-integration Commission (CORE) was established, intended to channel support for returning displaced people and refugees and to help demobilised soldiers to re-integrate into civilian life. Initially, the argument that ex-combatants should get special attention was dismissed, on the grounds that thousands of civilians deserved at least equal support. But ex-soldiers' frustrations sometimes boiled over into riots and looting, as they raided warehouses where aid supplies, meant for more vulnerable groups, were stored. In some places aid workers were held at knife point until they released supplies.

Eventually the international donors decided to defer plans for long-term training, credit, and employment and to pool resources for an 18-month scheme to augment veterans' compensation pay. As donors admitted, they were buying time for peaceful elections.

Practical problems

Demob pay was to be disbursed in monthly instalments, paid through the thinly spread, rural banking system. Donors pledged US$20 million to the scheme, with compensation packets to start at the legal minimum wage, worth US$15/month, ranging to a top pay worth US$120/month. The figures were not adjusted for inflation, then running at about 50 per cent per annum. Ex-combatants going home to remote rural areas had to spend much of their pay on bus fares to the bank.

CORE had promised ex-combatants 'special programmes and support ... access to arable land ... and access to work and training'. Some demobbed soldiers did find training or work: for example, through one project 20 ex-soldiers in Niassa learned carpentry, nine others found work as fishers in Tete, and ten were employed at an hotel in Inhambane.

Antonio Augustinho was trained as a mechanic before he was drafted into the army in 1984. Demobilised ten years later, he now says, 'A soldier's life is useless. I never want to go back to it.' He could find no work in his old trade, but finally got a job with 24 other ex-soldiers, helping to rebuild the road from Nipepe District of Niassa to Cuamba town.

Yet such opportunities proved the exception rather than the rule. Ex-soldiers who were trained in starting small businesses found that they had no credit facilities, and that their compensation pay could not be used as start-up capital, because the banks had too little cash to pay them in a lump sum. The Mozambican Association of War Demobilised (AMODEG), created on the eve of the Peace Accord to represent the interests of all ex-combatants, complained that hundreds of its members had submitted project proposals to donors, but only a handful were ever approved.

Despite their post-war problems, or maybe even because of them, ex-fighters often led the way towards personal reconciliation. One of the first signs that peace had broken out in 1992 was fraternising between former enemy soldiers, who were soon playing football together, swapping cigarettes and war stories. In the months and years that followed, they embarked on common ventures, including business deals and even a political party.

A group of ex-soldiers working on a road-reconstruction programme in Niassa Province

JENNY MATTHEWS/OXFAM

Defence systems down

Peace talks between the government and RENAMO resulted in the unusual deal that both their opposing armies should be completely dismantled, and a new entity created in their place. Promoted as a voluntary, professional new army, the Armed Defence Forces of Mozambique (FADM) was planned to have 30,000 members, drawn half each from either side. Britain, Portugal, and France offered help with military training to upgrade professional skills and integrate the ex-enemy troops.

But soldiers voted with their feet. Most ex-combatants, given the choice, opted out of military life. Although the Peace Accord decreed that elections should not be held until the new army was fully formed, in the event by polling day the FADM had a mere 11,403 members, three quarters from the government's side and one quarter from RENAMO's smaller force. Not all were willing recruits: some ex-RENAMO soldiers admitted that they had been ordered to join. Not all volunteers stayed in: some ex-FRELIMO officers backed out when they found that salaries and conditions were no better than before. After the elections, few creditors seemed willing to put more money into a force recruited on a questionable basis, whose future role was still poorly defined. Worse, the new army gained a reputation for indiscipline and disorder, after riots and clashes with police over apparently petty issues.

Eventually in 1995, President Chissano appointed an ex-FRELIMO General as Chief of Army Staff, and an ex-RENAMO General as his deputy. Thus ended the dual command structure that had characterised the FADM. The President called on his new chiefs to discipline the troops so that they would earn the respect of civilians.

The Ministry of Defence was put under civilian control for the first time ever. It had to negotiate a new role for the defence force. With the end of civil war, there was no foreseeable threat to national security, either from a newly democratic South Africa or from other regional neighbours or foreign military forces. In any case, Mozambique's borders are too long to be protected by a conventional force, save at tremendous expense. It was not clear what the new army ought to be doing.

Legacies of war

After the Peace Accord, the country was riddled with illegal firearms and populated by thousands of desperately poor people, many of whom were trained in how to use them. Part of the ONUMOZ mandate was to take the weapons of war out of circulation. It notably failed to complete the task. The Cease-Fire Commission (CCF), responsible for confiscating illegally held weapons, met with only limited success.

Soon after ONUMOZ withdrew, violent crime and robberies began to soar. It was worst in urban areas, where the penniless and desperate rubbed shoulders with the rich, and on Mozambique's key international highways, where traders plied their goods down long, empty stretches of road. Even the Minister of Interior admitted that crime was so bad that 'before you set out somewhere these days, you have to pray twice that you'll arrive'.

Insecurity in Mozambique was furthermore a worry to neighbouring states across its porous borders, through which guns, drugs, stolen cars, and other illicit items flowed with ease. Improving the efficacy of the police became a key aim of the government, and one which donors were increasingly ready to back.

Landmines: a bitter harvest

Long after the end of civil war in Mozambique, the number of war casualties continued to grow.

The first landmine exploded in Mozambique on 14 June 1965. Over the next thirty years, hundreds of thousands of devices, strewn throughout the country, would claim some 10,000 victims, mostly civilians. Landmine clearance was the least successful aspect of the ONUMOZ peace operation. 'Anti-personnel devices' continue to kill and maim in a country classed alongside Afghanistan, Angola, and Cambodia as one of the world's worst-affected nations.

Mines were planted by FRELIMO freedom fighters and their Portuguese adversaries; by RENAMO and its Rhodesian and South African backers; by Tanzanian troops supporting FRELIMO; by Malawians; and doubtless by Zimbabweans.

Most of the devices were manufactured in the former Soviet Union or Eastern Europe, some of them recycled from Zambia or Angola via Rhodesia or South Africa, to Mozambique. Other mines were made in the United Kingdom, Belgium, China, France, Italy, Portugal, the United States, Rhodesia/Zimbabwe, and South Africa.

RENAMO used landmines extensively to sabotage the economy and isolate government towns and garrisons. According to human-rights researchers, the guerrillas used mines to target civilian populations, to block major supply routes and rural tracks, and as an ambush device. The government laid mines to protect key economic installations, around towns and villages where RENAMO was expected to attack, and along its borders with South Africa and Malawi.

Landmine maps at the end of the war were hopelessly incomplete, especially from RENAMO. The United Nations began with a strategy of de-mining along main roads which, it argued, must be made safe for the delivery of food aid to needy populations and for returning refugees to travel down. But post-war surveys showed that the vast majority of mine accidents occurred off the main roads on bush paths, at water sites, under trees, and in the fields where returnees were trying to plant again.

Steeped in controversy, the UN de-mining programme was delayed for over a year by in-fighting among various UN agencies and wrangling with the contractor. Eventually, a British consortium company formed by Lonrho and Royal Ordnance won the UN's biggest landmine-clearance contract so far: US$4.8 million to clear 2,000 km of road. It sub-contracted the physical work to Mechem of South Africa — a company which was formerly part of the apartheid state's defence industry and itself a producer of landmines, some of which were possibly planted in Mozambique.

Fortunately, other de-mining initiatives were already under way, sponsored by foreign governments. Norwegian-trained

At 2 pm on 29 October 1993, two men trying to rebuild a bridge over Nampaua River, Niassa Province, walked off into the forest to relieve themselves. One of them, 21-year-old Carlito Augosto, stepped on an anti-personnel mine. His leg was blown off at the knee and he suffered severe injuries to the groin, abdomen, and arm. It was 6.30 pm before workmates got him to Cuamba hospital, 50 km away. Carlito was dead on arrival.

Mozambicans were successfully de-mining in northern Tete Province. In Zambezia, former British army soldiers were working with Halo Trust, in support of aid programmes funded by British NGOs. Training four local de-mining teams, in 15 months Halo cleared 1,000 landmines, 8,000 items of unexploded ordinance (mortar shells, rockets, bombs, etc.), and 57,000 items of small-arms ammunition. This was merely scraping the surface of the problem.

More important than how many mines were taken out of the ground, however, was how much space had been handed back to local people, by making them feel secure. The mere suspicion of mines can put fields, schools, water points, roads, tracks and other vital resources out of use.

Halo team supervisor, Antonio Albino, was a primary-school teacher until RENAMO captured him. When he eventually escaped, he resigned from his job. 'The war was too hot: it was too dangerous to be a teacher.' Since the end of the war, he has contributed to education in a new way, de-mining around an ex-army barracks with his team so that the building can be used again — as a school. Antonio says, 'I was nervous at first, but now I enjoy my new job. I can dismantle and destroy any mine. It's a way to improve things for people.'

New limbs, new lives

As mine-clearance edges ahead, thousands of victims, maimed for life, are thrown back on their own resilience and resources.

Mozambique has three prosthesis clinics nationwide, fitting injured people with new limbs. The Quelimane clinic in Zambezia was set up with help from the Red Cross in 1986 and treats around 20 patients each month. It could serve more, but most disabled people have trouble finding money and transport to reach the clinic.

Two national organisations are trying to help them: the Mozambican Association of Disabled People (ADEMO) and the Mozambican Association of Disabled Soldiers (ADEMIMO). They aim to help their members get medical care and a livelihood. In Gurue, for example, a small tailoring business gives ADEMO members a profession, an income, and a new sense of worth. ADEMO president Farida Gulamo argues that new legislation is needed, to define government responsibility in caring for disabled people.

ADEMO and ADEMIMO are part of an active campaign urging Mozambique's government to sign Protocol II of the International Weapons Convention,

A prosthesis clinic for the victims of landmines in Quelimane

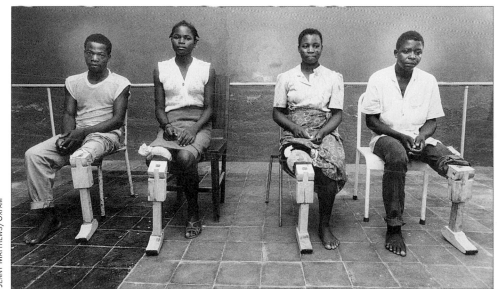

JENNY MATTHEWS/OXFAM

21

restricting the manufacture and use of landmines. In June 1995, ADEMO represented Mozambique at an international conference in Cambodia, where organisations from 35 countries sought strategies 'Towards an International Ban' on landmines. It addressed the launch of the 'Ceasefire Campaign', lobbying South Africa's government on the landmines issue.

Using radio, theatre, music shows, and vigils, campaigners inside Mozambique gathered 100,000 signatures on a petition to their government, asking it to ban landmines.

Bernando Juliao was just a boy of 11 when RENAMO attacked his school in Zambezia's Gurue District. The children fled, but when the guerrillas had gone, Bernando led back a team to clean up their classrooms. 'Just as I reached the school door, a mine blew up and I lost my leg,' he says. He was fitted with a false limb, but it soon became too short. He was 18 before he got another one.

Rita Mulanju, 25 years old, sits nursing her baby and talking about her farm at Incize Antoneta, where she grows her own food. Her crutches lie beside her. One day when she was 18, and walking back to her village, she trod on a landmine. It blew her leg away. Rita was carried to town in a mat and stayed three weeks in hospital. She married a farmer, but soon he joined the army. After the war he was called away for demobilisation, and never came back.

It was 1995 before Rita had the chance to reach the prosthesis clinic in Quelimane, where she was finally fitted with a new, metal leg. 'I still find it difficult to use,' she says. 'There are so many hills and rocks and streams where I live. I find it easier to farm my land on crutches.'

Creating a nation

FRELIMO gave up its monotheistic Marxist-Leninist philosophy in 1989, deciding to champion changes that elsewhere were sweeping one-party governments out of power. In 1990 FRELIMO introduced a liberal new constitution, declaring Mozambique to be a democratic state, permitting a market economy, and enshrining the rights to free expression and political choice.

The new constitution was preceded by nationwide public debates in all areas under government control. Popular opinion opposed two of the proposed reforms: privatisation of land, and the introduction of a multi-party system. The first objection was upheld. The second was quashed, on the grounds that the majority should not repress the minority. Moreover, pluralism was a necessary basis for peace.

Multi-party politics from scratch

No post-war election would have been meaningful without RENAMO — but when peace talks began in Rome, RENAMO was ill-prepared for a purely political contest. The mediators stepped in to help it 'transform from a guerrilla movement into a political party'. The transformation was three-fold: military, material, and political. RENAMO placed great emphasis on the material point. Its leaders argued that they could not exchange war for politics without housing, offices, cars, and fax machines.

ONUMOZ took the novel step of creating a Trust Fund to channel donations to RENAMO. With contributions from the European Union and several member countries, from the USA, South Africa, and Namibia, the Fund eventually totalled US$17 million. To all appearances, most of it was spent on hotel bills, new cars, and good living for RENAMO representatives serving on the peace-keeping commissions in Maputo.

ONUMOZ set up a second Fund, available to all registered political parties in Mozambique. The intention was to give a kick start to multi-party politics in a country whose deeply impoverished society had long been denied the right to form democratic organisations. The Fund attracted US$3.5 million, meant for spending on party offices, programmes, and propaganda, but not on election campaigning. For its part, the government disbursed nearly £16,000 worth of State money to each registered political party, and over £800,000 to share among the 12 presidential candidates. Donors admitted that some of the 17 registered parties which got a cut of the money were led by charlatans. They argued that it was a small price to pay for democracy.

Mozambique's first general elections

Created under the Peace Accord in January 1994, the all-Mozambican, all-party National Elections Commission (CNE) eventually won international praise for its performance. In the space of three months, it registered 6.4 million voters (over 80 per cent of the eligible population), set up some 8,500 polling stations nationwide, and organised the materials and some 50,000 staff to run simultaneous presidential and parliamentary elections for the first time in Mozambique.

With the demobilisation of troops formally complete and their rival armies abolished in September 1994, ONUMOZ gave the green light for elections to go ahead, on 27 and 28 October.

Despite a few ugly brawls, the election campaign ran smoothly overall. 'Article 19' of the London-based International Centre Against Censorship noted some problems: 'The major obstacle to freedom of expression in the rural areas during the election campaign remains the lack of freedom of movement in and out of territory controlled by RENAMO'. It noted 'a climate of fear among people living in RENAMO-controlled zones'.

Civic education, meanwhile, was relatively poor. The CNE was slow to organise and ONUMOZ late to disburse funds for educational materials. It was May before they started teaching a mostly illiterate population, virtually none of whom had seen a ballot box before, what secret voting with colourful bits of paper was all about.

'Article 19' monitored coverage of the campaign by the State-funded media, especially the national Radio Moçambique (RM). It found 'an inbuilt bias towards the ruling party', but reported that RM management and staff responded positively to criticism and that its coverage improved considerably during the campaign. The standard of the printed press, however, was found to be 'generally low and

extremely partisan, predominantly in favour of the ruling party'.

The worst moment of all was yet to come for ONUMOZ Chief Aldo Ajello. At around 11 pm on the night of 26 October, Afonso Dhlakama announced his withdrawal from elections, claiming that FRELIMO had prepared to win by fraud. If this was a last-ditch stand to force some concession of power ahead of the vote, it failed. Most RENAMO supporters did not get the message on time and went to the polls anyway. Dhlakama himself came under intense international pressure, especially from South Africa and Zimbabwe. By the second day of voting, he had changed his mind. In the end, he came a poor runner up, with 34 per cent of the vote against Chissano's winning 53 per cent.

His RENAMO party did much better, winning the vote in the five central provinces of Manica, Nampula, Sofala, Tete, and Zambezia. FRELIMO's massive vote in the south and extreme north gave it the edge, producing 129 seats in parliament against RENAMO's 112.

Only one other political group, the Democratic Union, qualified for seats in parliament by obtaining more than 5 per cent of the vote. Apparently this was a

A FRELIMO election poster half-concealed by a RENAMO poster

JENNY MATTHEWS/OXFAM

fluke: some voters mistook the UD for FRELIMO, owing to the way it appeared on the ballot card.

More than 3,000 international observers monitored the polling. Their overwhelming judgement was that the elections had been as free and fair as could be expected, given the immediate post-war context. With a turn-out of well over 80 per cent of registered voters, participation in Mozambique's first-ever multi-party elections was far greater than that of many European countries. They marked the end of the UN mandate. Above all, they signified a triumph for the Mozambican people.

Nonetheless, it was much less a vote for ideas and policies than, primarily, a vote for peace.

Which way now?

Not long after the fuss and bluster of elections was over, it looked as though Mozambique could soon go the way of other States in the region, remaining nominally pluralist but, in practice, rapidly returning to the one-party mould.

Its constitution attributes over-riding powers to the President, leaving parliament with a relatively weak role. Should parliament reject the government's programme, the President may dissolve it and call for fresh elections. The 250 deputies of Mozambique's first post-war parliament approved the FRELIMO executive's Five Year Plan of government, and its programme and budget for 1995, practically without discussion, and with only two votes against.

Outside parliament, at least temporarily, the host of minor opposition parties quickly sank out of view. RENAMO without the Trust Fund was soon in financial crisis — intensifying internal divisions that began with its 'transformation' from a guerrilla movement in the bush to a political party with an elite leadership in the capital city.

There may be a warning in the trend. Western donors and creditors created the conditions for multi-party elections, based on a purely Western model of democracy. Local traditions of organisation, such as vesting authority in community councils, were not taken into account. Meanwhile Mozambique's extreme economic dependence on foreign creditors left little space for competing ideologies. All parties had to accept the donor-promoted version of liberal democracy, or risk consigning their country back to poverty.

In such circumstances, it is a tribute to tolerance that regional and ethnic differences were not more decisive in the contest for power. The possibility remains, however, that they could become so in future.

The next phase in Mozambique's democratisation is scheduled for 1997, when its first-ever multi-party local elections are due. Under a law approved by parliament in 1994, the government planned a phased introduction of elected municipalities, starting with the largest cities and gradually spreading down to the rural districts.

One nation?

The country which FRELIMO inherited at national Independence in 1975 was deeply divided by indigenous tradition, colonial policies, and regional differences in its development. Within its boundaries, over 100 linguistic dialects were spoken, by matrilineal clans in the north and patrilineal peoples in the south. Religious faiths ranged from Animist to Christian to Muslim, with combinations of all three. Many of its inhabitants had never even heard tell of a Mozambican nation.

FRELIMO was still trying to promote the concept of a nation-state when fighting broke out. The war with RENAMO intervened to intensify existing divisions between different regions and even between neighbouring communities.

After the war, FRELIMO adopted 'National Unity' as one of the principal themes for its first elections campaign Achieving that goal, overcoming all the historical impediments of social and political differences, economic imbalances, and poor communications between different parts and peoples of the country, presents a monumental challenge.

Rebuilding broken lives

Throughout Mozambique, the war uprooted rural communities and tore families apart, robbing them of their loved ones, their ancestral lands, and their dignity.

When war came to the sprawling hillside village of Nahorro in northern Zambezia, many young people fled from the zone. Nahorro elders stayed on. They tell how RENAMO guerrillas took control of their land and lives, forcing them to grow food and build huts for the soldiers. 'We had to hide from government soldiers. We had no clothes, so we beat tree bark and used it to dress in,' say the elders. Then they were put to work on sabotaging the road, digging up tar with hand-picks. 'Whoever became exhausted was killed. Many people died by the roadside, and the land is littered with their bones.'

After the war, one by one, surviving members of Nahorro came back. The elders were overjoyed to see relatives and friends who they had thought were dead. But returnees say, 'When we came back, we found a great difference in Nahorro. Landmines had been planted, poverty was much worse, and our fields had returned to bush. We had to start everything afresh. It will take years, many years, to rebuild.'

The first Mozambicans to move home after the end of the war were the hundreds of thousands of internally displaced. Joanna Alfredo was among them. She left Nahorro before the war when her husband went to work on a sugar plantation in Luabo, leaving all her things with her mother. 'When RENAMO attacked Luabo, we fled and I had to leave everything, all my pots, even my water bucket. We settled in Chinde, but there was no work and we were forced to live on hand-outs, free food and soap. After the war, we were given free transport back to Nahorro. I just thank God that we reached home before my mother died. But all our things had gone and my heart bled for her, she was so poor.'

With free seeds and a hoe provided by a British aid organisation, Joanna started farming again. 'We have no news about my husband's job in Luabo, and anyway he is old now. We don't know what the future holds. All we can do is keep farming.'

The long trek home

As peace was established, a steady stream of refugees began flowing back into Mozambique, over the borders from Malawi, Zimbabwe, Zambia, Tanzania, Swaziland, and South Africa. The overwhelming majority were 'spontaneous returnees', travelling home by their own means, often on their own two feet, crossing mountains and rivers alone. Many refugee communities sent some of their men as scouts, to test out the route and size up the home situation before women and children followed on.

The office of the United Nations High Commissioner for Refugees (UNHCR) appealed for US$203 million to fund a three-year repatriation programme, described as its largest yet in Africa. It mediated agreements on the conditions of return between Mozambique and the countries that had played host to the refugees, provided limited transport, and set up services like health and water posts at returnee-reception points. The eventual return of an estimated 1.7 million refugees to Mozambique was little short of a miracle. Some 316,000 people were brought home through the UNHCR's official repatriation programme.

In southern Gaza Province, returnees who had fled from RENAMO attacks on their homes in Massingir reported that they were well received by the ex-rebels, who confirmed: 'The war is over.' Re-assured, they built new houses, not far from the ruins of their old ones. Only this time, they were not forced to live in communal villages. The government said they could return to the land of their ancestors.

Yet long after the war, and even after the elections, political control over parts of central Mozambique remained in dispute. The government struggled to extend its administration to RENAMO-controlled settlements in long-isolated areas of the bush. Throughout Mozambique, returnees would call on their local *regulos*, who still held the social authority to distribute land among village communities. Returnees to northern Mutarara District of Tete found themselves cut off from their former lands by politics and economic isolation. Pro-RENAMO *regulos* refused to let them go back to their farmlands, unless they renounced contact with government-controlled towns. But food aid and seeds were distributed from the towns.

Some returnees came back with the few possessions they had managed to carry away: a sewing machine, blankets, some chickens or a goat. Others had learned new skills while living in a refugee camp, like tailoring, carpentry, and knitting. A few came back richer than they had left, after farming or working abroad. But the vast majority came back with next to nothing, in urgent need of food, seeds, and tools to get started again.

Broken bridge, Ruace, Zambezia Province, 1995: an all-too-familiar scene in areas affected by the civil war

CARLOS MHULA/OXFAM

27

Thousands of children were orphaned or separated from their families during the civil war

JENNY MATTHEWS/OXFAM

Reunited

One day in 1988, 13 year old Julianna Makanara was kidnapped by RENAMO as she left her home village of Lioma in Zambezia Province to visit family nearby. When the war ended, her father made long trips on foot, seeking any information that might lead to her. In 1993, many Lioma children found their way back to the village from RENAMO camps nearby. But Julianna was not among them. Her family nearly gave her up for dead.

Then one day, six years after she had disappeared, Julianna's father saw a photograph of his daughter in the local administrator's office. Tears of joy streamed down his face. It was a recent photo, but Julianna looked just like her sister and there could be no mistaking. She was living at Alfazema, one of RENAMO's major bases in Zambezia during the war.

Julianna's photo was circulated to Lioma by the government's Accao Social (welfare department) with dozens of others, showing children lost, captured, or abandoned during the war. Accao Social began its 'family re-unification programme' well before the end of the war, using photographs and any family details the children could remember, to try to reunite them with at least some members of their extended families. With older children like Julianna, there was a good chance of success. Countless younger children could not tell where they came from or what their parents were called.

Three years after the end of the war, Accao Social had helped some 12,000 families to find each other again. But some 'lost' children were still appearing, while others will never find their families.

The dwindling of vast lands

Mozambican identity is engraved upon the land. The countryside bears the hall-marks of local history: the trees which commemorate a graveyard, the sacred mountain where rain-making rituals are performed, the dense bush where boys and girls are initiated into adult life. But the land is also marked by a long and repeated history of dispossession: through tribal conflict, colonial conquest, natural disaster, State removals, civil war, and now, again, through private enterprise taking over community land.

It is ironic that there should be conflicts over land in a vast and fertile country with some 80 million hectares of land and only 17 million people. Simple arithmetic suggests that there should be plenty for all. Of the 80 million hectares, however, fewer than half are suitable for farming, and only 18 million hectares are good for cultivation (rather than grazing). Some of that land is isolated from other resources. Along Mozambique's main rivers and international highways, near towns and along the borders with neighbouring countries, where water, communications, and markets exist, competition for land is often intense.

A two-tier system administers land in Mozambique: one governed by customary authorities and rules, the other by the State and its national constitution. Traditionally, land is distributed among the members of a rural community by the local chief, generally known as the *chef das terras* (land chief) or *regulo*. The chiefs' authority was brought into the service of the Portuguese colonial State, which allowed them local powers in return for collecting taxes and providing labour from the local population. The State could meanwhile allocate land to private

companies, Portuguese settlers, and colonial plantations.

After Independence, FRELIMO nationalised all land, under the slogan *Land Belongs to the People!* The *regulos* were officially divested of their powers. But peasants' hopes that their colonised land would be handed back to them were quickly dashed. The State took over and expanded agricultural estates, pushing local people to the margins. Meanwhile, thousands of rural people were herded into communal villages, first for political reasons as FRELIMO tried to 'socialise' the countryside, then for security reasons as the army either tried to defend them against guerrilla attack or, sometimes, tried to clear the bush of potential RENAMO supporters.

When drought compounded the effects of economic collapse, famine and spreading civil war forced literally millions of farmers from their lands, to internal refuge and over the borders into exile.

The end of civil conflict brought new hope to Mozambicans that, at last, they would regain their lost heritage. Tradition proved its resilience as land chiefs across the country successfully allocated land to hundreds of thousands of returnees, finally earning tacit recognition for themselves by the government. Yet even as refugees trekked home to the soils their ancestors had tilled, new conflicts over land were beginning to create yet another wave of displaced and disenfranchised people.

Who owns the land?

Just after national Independence, hundreds of small-scale farmers from the well-watered, fertile district of Chokwe in southern Gaza Province were moved off their lands and into communal villages. District land was thereafter largely occupied by State farms. Then in 1984, 1989-91, and 1992, large parts of the 33,000 hectares of State farmland were successively given to individual farmers. However, in many cases the beneficiaries were not the original farmers, but private commercial interests from outside Chokwe. Local small-holders, already forced to move by government policy and then by war, were once again pushed off their land.

Among the disinherited were a group of vociferous farmers. In 1993, they claimed they had been expelled from their lands by the Lomaco company, an agricultural venture jointly owned by the Mozambican State and the British-based multi-national, Lonrho. The farmers alleged that Lomaco had ploughed up their fields, cut down their trees, and destroyed their houses on some 4,000 hectares of irrigated land, to expand its own cotton production. Although they were promised compensation, said the farmers, this had never materialised.

At the time, Lomaco said it had reserved around 150 hectares of irrigated land for distribution to local peasant farmers, but the large number of competing claims had made it impossible to share the land out.

Such disputes are becoming more and more common. National law maintains that all land belongs to the State, which may concede land for commercial use for a certain length of time (usually 50 years). In 1987, a new clause was introduced specifically to protect small-scale farmers. It gave them the automatic right to use land they had traditionally farmed, and the right to obtain a land-use title deed. No trade in land, land concessions, or deeds was legally permitted. Nearly ten years after its introduction, the land-titles clause had done little but frustrate and disappoint small-scale farmers. Most were unaware of the law, or could not afford to get titles. Although the titles were 'free', they could be issued only for demarcated land — and getting your land marked out could cost a fortune.

The Rural Organisation of Mutual Support (ORAM), now a group of some 60 peasant farmer associations, was set up in 1992. One of its key objectives was to help members to obtain land-use title deeds. Financial support from international NGOs and church organisations enabled

Peasant farmers can have no security without legally recognised rights over their land

ORAM to pay all costs in full for over 80 applications to register land. Three years later, apparently due to bureaucratic delays and complications, the authorities had not yet allocated a single land-title to ORAM members. The few small-scale farmers of Mozambique who did obtain titles complained that they still had very little security.

Once the civil war was over, the Land Law became a shield for a rampant, completely uncontrolled market in land, thriving amid corruption and a bewildering plethora of competing land claims. Land was being parcelled out by local government bodies and by officials from the Ministries of Agriculture, Finance, Industry, and Mineral Resources. Some bits of land were given out three or four times over by different authorities; according to its own records, Mozambique had even given away bits of Tanzania.

Researchers claimed that a good number of the new concession-holders were mere speculators in land, with no intention of putting it to productive use. The principal losers were the small-scale farmers who lacked both legal knowledge and financial resources to protect their land rights.

Leased to the highest bidder

Refugees returning from South Africa to the wild and rocky terrain of Massingir District in Gaza were shocked to find white South Africans patrolling their home land. Returnees to Chimangue village said the Boers called them to a meeting, told them they had acquired all the surrounding land from the Mozambican government, and ordered local people to stop hunting for food. Village elders said they were stunned: 'The Boers made us suffer in South Africa, and now they order us about in our own homes.' The National Wildlife Department explained that Chimangue lies within 'Coutada 16', a game-rich area marked out in colonial times as a hunting reserve. In 1994 the Government gave a three-year renewable concession to a joint South African-Mozambican safari company, which now held the hunting rights.

The same year, public opinion was shocked at reports that the Ministry of Finance had signed a 'Protocol of Understanding' with MAHEDCO, the Maharishi Heaven on Earth Development

Company run by followers of Maharishi Yogi and his system of transcendental meditation. The protocol allowed MAHEDCO to set up its rural development project on an unspecified amount of 'unused' land in Mozambique. MAHEDCO's own publicity talked of occupying 20 million hectares. President Chissano is a keen practitioner of transcendental meditation and once attributed the success of the peace process to its harmonising powers.

The MAHEDCO furore eventually died down, leaving little trace — just as a new problem emerged. This time it seemed likely that the plan would be realised. In 1995, the Mozambican government entered into negotiations with South Africa over an amazing proposal by two Afrikaner farmers' unions in the Orange Free State and the Transvaal. A deal was sought to allow the mass migration of Afrikaner farmers to Mozambique, in a modern and rather more diplomatic repeat of the Great Trek which took them through South Africa as far as southern Mozambique in the nineteenth century.

Many Mozambicans feared for their national sovereignty, comparing the Afrikaner plan to Mozambique's earlier colonisation by Portuguese settlers. Many others, however, were in favour of the move, under certain conditions: as long as the Afrikaners were sent to virgin lands and not allowed to move anyone else off their territory, they said, the newcomers could bring trade and development to isolated areas.

By this time, virtually everyone agreed that the land law was not working. Many Mozambicans also complained that the government was not serious about attracting useful investors. It was only after winning general elections, however, that the government dared to tackle the problem of land law.

In 1995, a Permanent Land Commission was established and drew up the first-ever proposal for a National Land Policy for Mozambique. The key objectives were to simplify land administration and dampen the spreading fire of conflicts over the control and use of land. To these ends, the Commission recommended that all land should remain the property of the State, but that trade should be allowed in land-use titles — on condition that only Mozambican nationals could buy them. It recommended that customary land-rights systems and the role of traditional chiefs in allocating land should be recognised and integrated in the legislation, and it suggested marking out protective boundaries around peasant-farmer communities, for example by including all the members of a particular lineage group or clan.

Peasant-farmer associations said they welcomed the proposals, although their implementation seemed a long way off.

Small-scale farmers are the backbone of the economy of Mozambique

JENNY MATTHEWS/OXFAM

Assets of the earth and sea

Agriculture is the backbone of Mozambique's economy. Most of its people depend on their own small farms for survival. In times of crisis — civil war, drought, or flood — many thousands have been reduced to living on wild leaves and berries or, more recently, international food aid.

Yet Mozambique is blessed with vast areas of fertile terrain, which can produce enough food for the nation and even a surplus for export. The hardwood forests, cashew-nut trees, and cotton fields of the north give way to rice paddies and coconut groves on the central coastline. Maize, sugar cane, and citrus fruits all count among Mozambique's major market products. Traditional food crops include sorghum, cassava, sweet potato, beans, pumpkin, and ground-nuts.

Under Portuguese rule, Mozambicans provided cheap labour for settler farms and colonial estates, which raked in the profits from export crops. But low wages and seasonal work meant that most labourers' families had to grow their own food, spending their pay on taxes and basic items like soap and salt. In the north, peasant farmers grew cotton through the hated *chibalo* system of forced labour. Low incomes and excessive demands on labour meant that local small-scale farming could not be developed.

After Independence, Frelimo took over the colonial estates and much of the commercial network, which had collapsed after the exodus of Portuguese traders and shop-keepers. It put all its eggs in the basket of rapid, capital-intensive expansion on huge State-owned farms. From 1977 to 1984, over 90 per cent of investment in agriculture went to the State sector, as the government imported hundreds of new tractors and other agricultural machines. There was little left over for running costs, like buying petrol and fertiliser.

The 'party of peasants and workers' utterly neglected the peasants. Small-scale farmers were encouraged (or pushed) to form collective co-operatives,

Coconut palm in Pemba, Cabo Delgado Province
JULIAN QUAN/OXFAM

where everyone was meant to work together on communal fields. But they were not given extra resources, and most production co-ops failed. When the State farms also failed, largely due to lack of planning and managerial capacity, the 'family sector' of small-scale farmers could not meet the nation's food needs. As civil war in the countryside forced more and more farmers off their land, the situation became catastrophic.

In the widespread famine of 1983/84, over 100,000 people are said to have died of starvation. A tragedy of similar proportions, when drought hit all of southern Africa in 1990/92, was averted only by timely imports of international food aid.

From 1983, the government gradually adopted a new strategy of liberalising agriculture, starting by removing the fixed price of cabbages and moving on to the privatisation of State-owned farms. Almost all hope of post-war economic recovery in Mozambique has been pinned on reviving and expanding agricultural production.

In the first full year of peace (1992/93), agricultural production surged by an impressive 23 per cent, as the drought broke, the land was green again, and thousands of farmers flocked back to their abandoned fields. Yet long-term agricultural revival is far from assured. Without more support for small-scale producers, the risk looms large that Mozambique could remain a dependent nation producing nothing but primary commodities, playing host to a few colonial-style companies, while hundreds of thousands of peasant farmers struggle without success to emerge from subsistence-level production.

Cheia-Cheia

The lands of Chief Cheia-Cheia and his people lie on a dusty scrub-plain, dipping down through a silvery, sparsely-leafed forest to Lurio River. Tobacco plants and a few vegetables edge the river; papaya palms and cashew trees scatter the plain.

Chief Cheia-Cheia Nacarre tells how his ancestors led their Macua-speaking people down from the Namuli mountains on the other side of the river, after a long struggle for land with rival chief Mapiti. They settled in Nipepe District of Niassa Province in the north, in a place still called Cheia-Cheia.

From 1891 to 1929, their land was incorporated in the 100,000 square miles of territory which Portugal conceded to

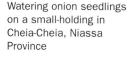

Watering onion seedlings on a small-holding in Cheia-Cheia, Niassa Province

34

Maize cobs piled high after the harvest

the mainly British-owned Nyassa Company. The company did little but collect taxes. Throughout colonial times, the Cheia-Cheia people paid tax to their rulers, usually in the form of sorghum or beans. The fourth Chief Cheia-Cheia died in a colonial prison, suspected of collaborating with FRELIMO guerrillas.

At the mercy of the rains ...
Agriculture in Cheia-Cheia still depends largely on the rains. When they are late, the village elders prepare flour from sorghum or rice and go down to the tree by the river marking their ancestors' graveyard. Clapping and singing, they sweep the grave site. Then the Chief rubs flour between his palms and asks the ancient spirits to pity their hunger and send them rain. This year it didn't work, but the elders are philosophical. 'A doctor can't always cure his patients,' they say.

The last harvests in Cheia-Cheia have been poor for another reason: most farmers have only recently returned from war-time refuge, some in Nipepe, others across the Lurio River, in Nampula Province.

'When RENAMO came here, we tried to hang on,' says Chief Nacarre, 'but every kind of killing took place. They would cut off people's heads while others were watching, and we were not allowed to bury the heads.' When the farmers fled, their huts and granaries burned behind them. They returned after the war to fields that had disappeared under bush.

The first external assistance they received was seeds and new tools. It was enough to make a start, but they were still at the mercy of irregular rains. The maize seeds they received were not very hardy. Now, with further help, Cheia-Cheia farmers are trying to re-diversify their crops, with short-cycle and drought-resistant varieties, such as short-season millet, mung beans, and the locally grown 'nachi'. These can be inter-cropped with the usual staples of maize, millet, and sorghum, but harvested early to get through the hungry season from February to May. By spreading their range of crops, local farmers are bringing stability back to their food supply; but they must sell cash crops to buy other basic goods, such as soap, clothing, and salt.

... and the mercy of the market
Trade in Nipepe District was paralysed by the civil war and is only gradually returning. One of the first traders back was Joao Fereira dos Santos (JFS), a

35

Ayecaia Muichi in her sunflower field: 'I may be old, but I'm still happy to try growing new things.'
JENNY MATTHEWS/OXFAM

Portuguese-owned cotton company operating in Mozambique since colonial times. At first people resented its return: older farmers bitterly remembered how they were forced to grow cotton under Portuguese rule. But some people were glad to see the company back. 'The colonials used to beat us to make us grow cotton,' says Joaquina Mako. 'Now for the first time, I'm growing it from choice.'

Cotton growing has advantages: JFS supplies seeds, technical assistance, and sacks, which are not discounted from the sale price until after the harvest is in. Perhaps most important, the company provides a guaranteed market for cotton. In return, JFS enjoys a buyer's monopoly.

Cotton is being revived as an export crop. In 1994, it accounted for more than one third of Mozambique's total export earnings. It is mainly grown by small-holders, who sell to companies owned jointly by the Mozambican State and any one of the 'big three' companies growing cotton in Mozambique since colonial times: JFS, Entreposto (with Portuguese capital), and Lonhro (with British capital). The price to farmers is fixed by discounting all service costs to the companies. The small-holders are paid whatever is left over from export sales. In 1995, this worked out at around £20 for an ordinary farmer's annual crop.

Other cash crops are harder to sell in Nipepe. Ex-soldier Adriano Morais launched into farming after the war, and soon his yard was piled high with maize cobs. No one came to Nipepe to buy them. So Adriano planned to transport his maize to the nearest town of Cuamba, over 250 km away. The State-owned Cereals Institute, ICM, has a branch in Cuamba, buying grain at a fixed price. ICM is meant to be a buyer of last resort, but its minimum price in practice acts as a maximum price. No one checks up on traders travelling out of Cuamba, so they can set whatever price they like. No one will cover Adriano's transport costs.

The Lurio river banks offer excellent soil for tobacco, while Cheia-Cheia produces abundant ground-nuts. But farmers in this isolated region must solve the marketing problem. Jose Laurenco grows tobacco and dries it in the sun, before rolling it up for sale. With 15 rolls of leaf on his head, he sets off on the two-day walk to his nearest market in Montepuez, Cabo Delgado Province: a trip he will have to make three times to sell all his tobacco.

Some enterprising farmers in Nipepe are trying new ways to add value to their crops and attract buyers into the district itself. Great-grandmother Ayecaia Muichi planted sunflower seeds for the very first time when she came home from refuge after the war. Receiving one kilo of free seeds, she gave half to her daughter and sowed the rest herself. The sunflowers took kindly to her field and grew strong and fast, until soon she had her own sackful of seeds for sale. She used the cash to buy new clothes, to replace the shoddy rags which her impoverished family had grown used to.

Ayecaia says, 'Before the war, I used to have so many things that I can't afford now.' One of them was cooking oil. The oil on sale in Nipepe now is imported from Malawi; transport costs push up the price to an impossible 18,000 meticais (c. £1.20) per litre. But Ayecaia may soon be consuming oil from her own fields. After the war, ex-soldier Alberto Jamo opened a small shop and the only bakery in Nipepe. His latest interest is in a simple, hand-operated press to squeeze oil from sunflower and sesame seeds. If he buys the press on hire-purchase, he reckons, he could soon be making a profit, while providing a service to local oil-seed growers. Traders from Cuamba might well make the trip to Nipepe, if there were edible oil for sale.

Wealth from the sea

Its sandy beaches shaded by palm trees and tangled mangroves, the Mozambican coast abounds with a rich variety of sea foods prized around the world, like prawn, crab, and lobster. Prawn exports to Europe, the USA, and Japan have long been Mozambique's biggest single source of hard currency (earning US$63 million of the total export income of US$165 million in 1994). Pirate trawlers from South Africa, Japan, Russia, and other countries haul in great shoals of fish from Mozambican waters, and the under-funded national maritime authorities can do little to stop them.

At the other end of the scale, fishing supplies valuable protein for the diet and cash for the pockets of many coastal peoples in Mozambique. The fishermen of Mocimboa da Praia, northern Cabo Delgado Province, set out to sea with their nets in little wooden boats, coming home with a catch of thin, silvery fish that turns the beach into a market place as locals rush down to buy it.

The women use simpler methods, wading out with a drag net, up to their chests in sea-water. Fisherwoman Fato Sulemane tells how she and her friends began fishing. They sewed together a string of *capulanas* (local cloths). A few hours spent wading in the bay, and their makeshift nets would be 'full, full, full'. Recently they acquired proper fishing nets, more effective and easier to use than *capulanas*. But now the women face growing competition, and fish stocks appear to be dwindling.

Mocimboa women are only part-time fishers: for six months of the year they move 60 km inland to the wet valleys of Antadora to grow rice — to eat, to sell, and to use in the traditional ceremonies of their Muslim, Kimwani culture. The men stay in Mocimboa, doing a little trade here and there. Although they don't produce the rice, Kimwani tradition dictates that they control its sale.

Walking wealth

Inland, Mozambican farmers generally keep livestock of some kind. On the gentle grazing plains of the south, before the war, local chiefs often counted their wealth and paraded their status in terms

Kimwani women fishing off the shore near Mocimboa da Praia

JENNY MATTHEWS/OXFAM

of cattle. Cattle were used not only for meat, but for ploughing, transport, and as a trading commodity. The usual way for a man to pay *lobolo* (bride price) was through a gift of cattle to his wife's family. So precious were cattle that their owners would often give them symbolic names, recalling their ancestors.

The bulk of Mozambique's cattle stock was wiped out in the civil war. Astronomical prices and complex importation laws have made restocking an arduously slow process. Cattle rustling back and forth over the borders with South Africa and Swaziland remains a serious problem, costing human lives. Infestation with tse-tse fly makes much of the centre and north of the country unsuitable for cattle. Here goats, pigs, ducks, and chickens are common, although their populations were also badly hit by the war.

Maria Acibo, of Boma village, Niassa, had many goats before the war. She feels so bitter at losing them all that she says she won't breed them again. Instead, she has started with pigs. Under a local loan scheme, she received a pair of pigs, on condition that she must give a pair of the first piglets to another Boma family. The new scheme adapts a traditional system where families and friends would lend animals to each other, helping to increase the local stock.

Maria (who also grows maize, sorghum, beans, oranges, and cotton and keeps chickens and ducks) hopes that pig-breeding will help her to earn enough money to buy blankets for the winter. Stoically, she says, 'The war is over. Only the lazy cannot hope to improve their lives.'

Plantation life

Elderly Zambezian, Armando Nsana, has worked at the coconut factory ever since he was a boy. From six in the morning till five at night, he and his workmates sit outside the furnaces cracking open baked coconuts, 1,500 of them each day. Their pay is worth little more than £6.00 a month.

Seasonal workers on the tea plantations of mountainous Gurue lead a similar life, straining their backs from dawn till dusk as they stoop over the low bushes to pick tea leaves, for less than thirty pence per day.

Three years after the civil war ended, many farming estates were still heavily decapitalised, unable to make a profit. Their workers, however loyal, received short shrift from employers who claimed that they had no money to pay them more than the slave-like wages on offer.

All State-owned farms have been privatised, and private agricultural concerns are seeking fresh investment capital. But attracting private investment is not all that easy, given Mozambique's record of insecurity, its bad roads, poor infrastructure, and unreliable communications. Access to cheap labour is still one of the key incentives used to attract potential investors in Mozambique.

A herd boy in Chicualacuala, Gaza Province
IAN BRAY/OXFAM

Roads to prosperity

Jenny Matthews/Oxfam

Mozambique's historical fortunes and misfortunes alike are deeply rooted in its geography. A thousand years ago its Indian Ocean coastline and deep sea-water ports attracted the Arab and Asian traders whose thriving commerce with the East eventually provoked the envious invasion of Portuguese adventurers.

Its easy access to maritime trade routes helped to make Mozambique a prime location for agricultural plantations and estates, from where sugar, tea, coconuts, tropical fruits, and other produce could be easily exported. As the Europeans shaped southern Africa into its present-day nation states, access through Mozambique's transport 'corridors' to the sea became an economic necessity for its hinterland neighbours, for which they were prepared to pay and even fight.

In the nineteenth century, British and Portuguese colonials battled hard for control of Delagoa Bay, now the site of the capital city and port of Maputo and still serving substantial trade from South Africa. On the eve of national Independence in 1973, the ports of Mozambique handled all of Malawi's export-import trade, two thirds of Rhodesia's, half of Swaziland's, and one fifth of South Africa's. The strategic significance and earning power of Mozambique's international trade routes to its mostly land-locked neighbours were a key factor in the historic neglect of its own north–south and domestic communications. To this day, most roads are unsurfaced, and only one major highway runs south–north up the country, while many areas of this vast country remain inaccessible by road.

When RENAMO began its war of destabilisation, roads and railway lines were a key target. By 1985, Zimbabwe was deploying 12,000 troops to protect its road, rail, and oil-pipeline corridor through central Mozambique to Beira port and in the Limpopo Corridor to Maputo, while Malawi had 400 soldiers in the northern Nacala Corridor.

Yet war-time sabotage and neglect put some 70 per cent of the national road network out of use. RENAMO mined roads, blew up bridges, and tore up rail-lines. FRELIMO soldiers made their own contribution, laying mines around settlements and strategic installations to keep the guerrillas away. Fear and neglect did the rest. Bush grew over the unused roads; rain washed bridges away. Countless thousands of Mozambicans were isolated in their own country, and over-land domestic trade ground to a virtual stand-still. There was no passable

Outspan oranges, transported by rail from South Africa for export from Maputo

Zimbabwean soldiers
guarding the Beira Line
during the civil war
KEITH BERNSTEIN/OXFAM

Peace Accord. There were then no usable roads leading out of the district. Huddled around the government administration offices in Nipepe, thousands of displaced people were dependent on food aid. Nobody knew how many others were living under RENAMO control elsewhere in the district, nor what condition they were in.

Manuel set out to find them. He wrote to RENAMO leaders to say that his aid agency would assist local civilians, if it could find where they were. Suspicious at first, eventually RENAMO sent guides who led Manuel on his 50cc motorbike through overgrown bush to the isolated interior. Here he found thousands of people, producing a little food, but lacking practically all other commodities. Many were virtually naked, or dressed in tree bark.

Their first request was for help with clothes. Soon after, some 200 civilian 'couriers', escorted by an armed RENAMO guard, came to Nipepe town to collect a donation of clothes. They carried the clothes on their heads on the long and exhausting walk home through the bush.

Gradually, RENAMO gained trust in Manuel's agency, grew more confident of its own contact with government areas, and agreed that roads through the district should be re-opened. The rebels called on the traditional chiefs, who organised their communities. By hand, they cleared new roads to the heart of the district. Assistance in the form of clothes, seeds, and tools began to flow through. With time, seed sellers and cotton buyers followed on, as the aid routes once again became trade routes. Across the country, new settlements sprang up along the roadside as the national highways and byways came back into use. Marketeers and wandering traders came back to the villages, and the wheels of domestic trade began to creak into action.

highway linking the north to the south of the country. Many districts could be reached only by plane.

Efforts to re-open the roads and get goods and people in circulation again were among the first initiatives which eventually brought peace to Mozambique. When severe drought struck in 1991, the International Red Cross and United Nations agencies persuaded both sides in the war to open 'corridors of peace', allowing food aid through to the needy. Reconstructing access routes became a channel for building peace and re-integrating war-divided peoples.

What a difference a road makes

Aid worker Manuel Almeida first reached Nipepe district, Niassa Province, by plane, shortly after the signing of the

Mending roads, mending lives

Even before the end of the war, rebuilding roads had become one of the nation's top economic priorities. With heavy backing from the World Bank, Mozambique drew up a five-year programme to rebuild the network. Mozambique soon secured loans to fund most of the US$860 million needed to implement it.

Road rebuilding began in all of the country's ten provinces, with priority given to reconstructing surfaced roads before they could deteriorate beyond repair. The work depended heavily on imported equipment, raw materials, and expertise. The programme was well under way when the World Bank apparently changed track and began to question the wisdom of such a costly enterprise, building roads that Mozambique alone would be unable to maintain. Its new suggestion was that international highways could be rented out to private companies, who would maintain them by using the income from toll charges. Meanwhile, locally quarried rock and labour-intensive methods could be used to rebuild minor roads that could then be easily maintained.

Rehabilitation of the main road to Nipepe from Niassa's economic capital of Cuamba, some 255 km away, began in 1993. Local labour and materials were used to rebuild first the bombed and burned bridges and then the road. Basic rehabilitation, employing up to 300 local workers, was followed by a road-improvement phase, to cut back the bush, open rain-water drains at the side of the road, and mend the pot-holed surface.

After ten years of complete paralysis, in 1994 traffic to Nipepe started up again. The results were remarkable. In little over two years since the roadwork began, Nipepe-sede was transformed from a stagnant back-water without a single shop or passing trader to a gently humming centre with growing potential. A small market had sprung up and two or three shops re-opened, while 'banana beer' from Nampula Province and tinned sardines and biscuits from Malawi were on sale. A lorry came down from Cuamba, looking for trade.

Julietta Mwanatela has lived all her life in central Zambezia Province, where her parents once worked on the tea plantations. Long ago, her mother taught her how to make clay pots. Julietta gathers clay from the river, pounds it soft, and gently shapes it with her hands. With a thin strip of metal, she scrapes off the excess clay; then she uses a cloth to smooth the rim, and a little broken piece of china tile to pattern the moist surface. Then she lights a wood fire under her simple oven. It takes two to four days for the pots to dry. Big pots, she sells for 6,000 mt each (around 40 pence).

Since the war ended and traffic began to flow past her roadside home in Alto Molocue, Julietta's trade is booming. Already she has plastered her wattle and daub house, using profits from her pot sales. Now she hopes to earn enough money for doors and windows.

Carlos Mhula/Oxfam

The economy: painful choices

Since Independence in 1975, national economic policy has taken Mozambique from a heavy-handed, soviet-style, planned economy, through liberalisation to what some economists have described as a savage form of 'raw capitalism'.

FRELIMO's original ambition was to spread wealth to the poor and raise living standards for everyone. But bitter experience proved that the early strategy for rapid economic development through State control of everything from the price of cabbage to workers' pay could simply not be realised. FRELIMO lacked the resources — technical, financial, and human — to carry out its ten-year development plan, and to run all the farms, factories, shops, and service institutions which it took over at Independence.

The plan relied too heavily on 'big projects', requiring imports that Mozambique could not afford. Eventually, the State was footing huge bills to run businesses and pay workers whose out-put covered only a fraction of the costs. By 1985/86, production levels were around half those achieved on the eve of Independence. Goods of all kinds disappeared from the shops, urban streets filled up with bread queues, and farmers stopped selling crops, because there was nothing to buy in exchange. Mozambique began its long slide into debt.

The result of trying to control the entire economy was that much economic activity went on through the back door on the illegal 'parallel market', where prices ran riot.

Liberalising the economy

As hunger began to bite, liberalisation started to creep in. In 1985, fixed prices for fruit, vegetables, and chickens were the first to be abolished. Soon after, Mozambique agreed to try to cure its economic ills by using the standard prescription of the world's most powerful finance doctors, the International Monetary Fund (IMF) and the World Bank. In 1987 it introduced its liberal Economic Reform Programme (PRE), later renaming it PRES when a social component was added, offering minimum assistance to the 'vulnerable' poor.

The key objectives of PRE were to balance Mozambique's budget and make it credit-worthy in the eyes of Western financiers. This meant cutting back the State's role in planning and production, leaving the former to 'market forces' and the latter to private enterprise.

Implementing PRE/S has included removing all fixed prices and government

Maputo City, 1995
JENNY MATTHEWS/OXFAM

subsidies on food; imposing tight restrictions on State spending and credit; liberalising exchange rates (the value of the national currency against the US dollar plummeted from 40 metical in 1986 to approximately 10,000 mt in 1996); privatising State-owned enterprises; ending government monopolies in education, health-care, and other services; and introducing charges for services such as health care that used to be free.

Initially, production rose under PRE. The World Bank argued that it would have continued to rise, were it not for 'external factors' such as civil war, drought, and worsening terms of trade for key Mozambican exports on the international market. Yet these conditions were intrinsic to Mozambique's economy.

Although post-war growth rates have been more encouraging, by 1994 production *per capita* was no higher than it had been in 1986. National manufacturers produce such things as processed foods and drinks, batteries, tyres, electrical goods, cloth, metal products, and construction materials. These days they complain that tight credit and liberal import regulations, added to heavy taxes, prevent them from competing with foreign producers and much less with the sprawling market of illegally imported goods that escape customs duty.

According to popular wisdom, the most remarkable change brought about by liberalisation is that once, no one had much; now, most people have nothing — while a few have it all. Minimum monthly wages in 1995 were just 105,000 mt (c. US$10) for agricultural workers. Most people rely for survival on their own food production and petty trade. Only a handful of people (usually with good political connections) are acquiring wealth, either earned by legal means, or obtained from misused aid funds and smuggling rackets. Maputo city is resplendent with the luxury houses, Mercedes cars, and haute-cuisine restaurants frequented by the newly ostentatious elite of politicians and business people.

A stall in Maputo: empty Coca-Cola bottles for sale
CARLOS MHULA/OXFAM

Informal trade in action

The streets of Mozambique's major towns are lined with cardboard boxes and old sacks among the rubbish and the passing feet. On these humble stands, hundreds of hawkers display their wares: cigarettes from South Africa, charcoal, cabbage leaves, rough sugar for sale by the handful. In the market places, on the street corners, in back yards, untold informal transactions take place, involving more or less legally acquired goods.

While registered traders complain that they can't afford to pay government taxes, most are rumoured to be secretly selling out of their back doors on the informal market. The post-war government has promised to review its long list of cumulative taxes on trade, and investigate the problem of providing much-needed credit for small-scale enterprise.

Depending on aid

Mozambique is one of the most indebted countries in the world. In 1992 some 80 per cent of its State budget was financed by foreign aid, not to mention the numerous donor-funded projects not covered by government plans; the figure in 1995 was still 60 per cent of the State budget (90 per cent of the investment budget). The overall amount of foreign debt (US$5.4 billion in 1994) may seem small in international terms, but is huge when set against national earnings. Every Mozambican carries a debt of some US$300; the annual average income per head was US$80 in 1994.

This extreme dependence puts Mozambique in hock to its donors and financiers. The extent of its national sovereignty remains in question.

Can Mozambique manufacture its way out of trouble?

In the last days of colonial rule, Mozambique was the tenth most industrialised country in Africa. Beyond its agro-processing industry, it boasted chemical factories, textiles and mechanical engineering industries, coal mining, hydro-electric power-generation, ship-yards, and light manufacturing plants. However, the industrial sector has never overcome its heavy dependence on imports.

Industry was one of the sectors worst hit by war, which disrupted production of raw materials in the countryside, interrupted energy supplies, and destroyed supply and marketing routes. After the war, decapitalised national industry is still the worst-performing sector of the economy, its out-put in long-term decline.

Mozambique pinned strong hopes for industrial revival on agro-industry and on mining industries; its resources include coal, marble, gold, precious gems, mineral sands, and rare earth metals. It also counted on developing its energy resources, such as the hydro-electric power dam at Cabora Bassa in northern Tete Province, and its vast natural gas fields at Pande in the south. In line with the Economic Reform Programme, the government hoped also to develop tourism and attract fresh private investment through setting up 'Export Processing Zones', where producers for export are exempt from virtually all customs duties and taxes.

Neither FRELIMO's socialist plan nor the liberal PRE, however, has so far managed to create a vigorous market of national trade and enterprise, able to supply the domestic market and add substantial value to the nation's exports.

Mozambique's industrial future could thus depend on securing development capital from foreign investors, while trying to ensure that some of the profits stay at home. With its limited bargaining power, this may not be easy. In 1995, for instance, US government officials threatened to cut aid to Mozambique, unless it signed a major gas deal with American company ENRON.

Africa's largest hydro-electric power dam: Cabora Bossa, Tete Province

At the end of the rivers

From great rivers to tiny streams, Mozambique is rich in waterways. Springing from Angola's border with Zaire, the great Zambezi River crosses central Africa, thundering over the Victoria Falls to Zimbabwe and into northern Mozambique, fuelling Africa's largest hydro-electric power station at Cabora Bassa, before undulating down through Zambezia Province to the sea. The 'great, grey, greasy Limpopo' River waters southern Gaza Province, Mozambique's once-productive 'bread basket'. A myriad rivers and streams flow down from the hilly interior to the Indian Ocean coast.

None the less, some parts of this vast country remain perennially barren and dry, while water supplies to the south may be drying up permanently. Nationwide, most Mozambicans have no control over their water resources, remaining at the erratic mercy of floods, irregular rains, or drought.

At regional level, Mozambique's main water problem is its position at the receiving end of rivers which mostly have their source, and gather strength, in neighbouring countries. Some neighbours, like South Africa and Swaziland, are rapidly diverting the rivers to supply their own populations and fields. Nowadays the waterways often run dry before they reach Mozambique, whose southern terrain grows ever more parched.

Λ dried-up canal in Chokwe, Gaza Province

A river used to run through it

Small-scale farmer Talita Ndhlovu fled from her home in Mapulanguene on the border with South Africa during the civil war. When she came back from refuge in the South African Transvaal, she found that her farmlands had become too dry to yield anything. She was forced to build a little shack and camp on the banks of Mwenedzi River, which rises in South Africa. Although the river is now no more than a trickle, at least she can dig in its bed to collect a few cupfuls of water. Talita says that many Mozambican refugees who returned to Mapulanguene turned around and left again, once they saw there was no more water.

Mozambican attempts to secure a guaranteed water supply by means of international accords have met with little success. Although it sits on a Tripartite Committee with South Africa and Swaziland which is meant to negotiate shared use of water in the Incomati River basin, Mozambique has scarcely managed to uphold its interests. Over the border, dam-building projects continue apace. Water authorities in Mozambique explain, 'It's not that our neighbours don't consult us: they do. It's just that we have no bargaining power, so they end up doing what they want to, whether we like it or not.' Mozambique has further spoiled its own case, by failing to produce a scientific report to prove that its river-water levels are falling.

Water from the gods

The Kimwani elders of Ibo Island in northern Mozambique dance the 'Nacuale' rain dance for three days. On the morning of the fourth day, just after the sun rises, local people bring their contributions of food and traditional drink, tobacco, incense and a candle, and take them to a baobab tree. Here at the tree, where people say their ancestors used to live, they place their offering at the roots and tell the spirits, 'We have danced for rain, and we have brought the things you like.' Then they ask the ancestors' spirits for rain. 'And then it will rain, with certainty,' say the elders.

There seems to be an even more remote chance of success for international negotiations to share the great Zambezi River waters among the ten countries through which it passes.

The post-war government has gone ahead with plans to turn some of Mozambique's white elephants into useful, if not particularly economic, investments. Work to rehabilitate the Massingir dam in Gaza Province, finished in 1977 complete with technical faults, was expected to start in the late 1990s with US$80 million in financing from the African Development Bank. Abandoned by its Italian architects in 1991, the Corrumana dam in Maputo Province was still awaiting final touches, such as proper gates, in 1995, when it watered only 3,000 hectares of irrigated land, compared with its estimated capacity to serve 225,000 hectares.

Catching water on the hilltops

Every morning before dawn on the northern Mueda Plateau, scores of women begin their long journey down to the river and back, a round trip of 14 kilometres. The trek home is slow, as women trudge up the steep mountain slope, balancing 20-litre buckets of water on their heads. Many complain of swollen legs and sore backs.

Rains fall regularly on the hill-tops of Cabo Delgado's Mueda Plateau, where the land is fertile and green. Yet the rain-water quickly runs off the hard rock under the top-soil to the valleys below, leaving the Makonde people of the plateau with nothing nearby to drink or wash in.

After Independence, the new FRELIMO government made a special effort to improve water supply to the plateau, as a reward for Makonde people who had given so much support to its liberation struggle. Construction of an elaborate piped-water system, pumping up-hill from five rivers or streams, began in 1977. It was meant to serve 52 villages, but there was never enough diesel and engine parts. At the end of the pipeline, the villagers of N'toli say they have not seen a drop of piped water in the last ten years.

Now a grandmother, N'toli villager Njelenda Tiago played her part in the fight for national independence, during which the villagers joined FRELIMO in their fight against the Portuguese. Njelenda regularly gave flour to a messenger, who took it to the guerrillas, until she herself was captured and taken to a colonial jail.

'When FRELIMO came into power we were very happy, because FRELIMO is our party. We also thought this would mean improvements in our lives, such as local shops and a water supply,' says Njelenda. 'Something was done — but not enough,' she adds. With rising prices and continued maintenance problems, N'toli people see little hope of restoring the piped-water system. Much of its equipment has been put to other use or stolen.

Too old to make the trip herself, these days Njelenda sends her grand-daughter down to the river for water, when she is not too busy cooking, cleaning, or fetching firewood. 'With this lack of water, we all live in suffering,' she says. 'Look how dirty I am: I rarely manage to get a bath.'

It was the women of a pottery co-operative in N'toli who first saw a simple way to improve things. Some had seen rain-water catchment cisterns in Tanzania, and believed that a similar system could serve their needs. With financial support from an NGO and the help of Kenyan technicians, a rain-water catchment project began in N'toli. The district authorities offered transport, while local people helped with fetching stones and clearing a site to build the new facilities.

It's a strange-looking set-up. Rain-water is caught on a large slab of concrete that looks like a playground without children. From here it runs naturally down-hill, into a series of storage tanks. A local water committee controls the use of a tap at the front, meant to serve the community for several months each year until the stored water runs out.

The system is not perfect. Some of the first tanks to be built do not completely fill up, and some leak. When rains are poor, the stored water is used up after a couple

Njelenda Tiago: 'When water is in the tanks, we are very happy, healthy people.'

JENNY MATTHEWS/OXFAM

of months. None the less, N'toli villagers say the project is experimental and the water they do manage to 'catch' has changed their lives. 'When water is in the tanks, we are very happy, healthy people. We can take baths and practically manage to cure our illnesses,' exclaims Njelenda.

The Water Committee charges 500 meticais per 25 litres of water. After less than a year in operation, the Committee opened a savings account at the nearest bank with its accumulated income of 3.3 million meticais. They hope to use it to keep improving their water supply.

Source of hope

In 1980, only six per cent of Mozambique's rural population had safe water sources. Despite well-building efforts through the National Rural Water Supply Programme (PRONAR), by the mid-1990s some 70 per cent of rural dwellers were still dependent on unprotected water sources of dubious quality. The advent of peace has encouraged local communities in their initiatives to improve access to clean water.

Ida Martins, mother of nine from Ruace in Zambezia Province, feels there is little joy left in her life. She once worked on a State farm, where her husband was a tractor driver, and 'then I had many beautiful things'. Everything changed when RENAMO guerrillas destroyed the farm and captured Ida and her family, forcing them and other workers to march for many days to their Gorongosa headquarters, carrying guns and stolen goods from Ruace. 'We fared very badly on the march. Whoever was weak was killed. They even tore the babies off women's backs and threw them into the bush,' Ida tells, still grieving. Eventually the Martins family escaped from Gorongosa and made their way home. 'It's hard for me to talk about how I felt when we arrived. There was nothing left. We had to start life from scratch again.'

Ida says her life is little better since the Peace Accord. 'The State farm has not started up again. We have no paid employment: we just survive as best we can.'

Yet one thing has improved. 'I was always an active person at local women's meetings, and that's why I was chosen to join the Water Committee,' says Ida. Until recently, most people in Ruace had a narrow choice of water supply: either they could fetch it from the muddy river, where all and sundry would bathe and do their washing; or they could queue from early morning into the late afternoon to fetch water from the only well in the whole community. 'There was no hygiene and many illnesses came from the bad water,' says Ida, who lost four of her own children to disease.

Since the Water Committees were established after the civil war, five new wells have been built in Ruace. Committee member Fatima Pedro adds, 'Water is always available now; there are no more long queues, which gives us more time for cooking, cleaning, and farming.'

Washing clothes and collecting water from a muddy river in Ruace, Zambezia Province

CARLOS MHULA/OXFAM

Education: hungry minds

Next to the ruins of the old concrete school building in Natili in Niassa Province stands a humble new construction of thin sticks plastered over with brown earth. After the civil war, parents returning from refuge to Natili built two simple classrooms so that their children could go back to school.

Domingos Paulino is one of the new pupils. At 10 years old, he has only just started First Grade. 'During the war I was afraid of going to school, in case fighting started while I was there and I couldn't get back to my family,' Domingos says quietly. His fears seemed justified when the old Natili school was destroyed.

Now that teaching has started in the new, community-built school, Domingos is keen to work his way up to Grade Six. His parents are cautious, though: they can barely afford the pencils, books, and school clothes he will need. Thousands of children in Mozambique are in a similar situation. Indeed, they are the lucky ones.

Some fifty per cent of school-age children nationwide cannot find a place in education at all.

Colonial neglect ...

Unlike British colonials, who saw some advantage in educating a cheap African labour force, the poorer Portuguese took no such pains. The colonial State in Mozambique preferred a policy of exclusion, implemented through a two-tier system. While the State provided superior schooling for the children of settlers and the tiny minority of *assimilados*, African education was entrusted to rural missionaries, principally those of the Catholic Church. Few Mozambicans graduated beyond primary education. All teaching was in Portuguese; fees were high and so were failure rates.

When the Portuguese fled in 1975, over 90 per cent of the Mozambicans they left behind were unable to read or write. The

Schoolchildren sweeping the street outside a war-damaged building, Pebane District, Zambezia Province

SARAH ERRINGTON/OXFAM

49

country had barely a handful of university graduates. Educating the population is still one of the biggest challenges facing its post-war government.

... revolutionary fervour

Education has been a top FRELIMO priority since its early years. Its attempt to 'educate the masses' began in the so-called liberated zones of the guerrilla struggle, where children who could read and write were recruited to help teach those who could not. Adult literacy classes were very popular.

After taking power, FRELIMO rapidly expanded the national education network. Mission schools were nationalised alongside all other education facilities. The new government raised literacy levels to 25 per cent within a mere five years. Colonial school-teachers were expelled and young Mozambicans were called upon to take their places, sacrificing their own education. Schools and the teachers who ran them quickly became a symbol of much that was admired in FRELIMO. They also became a target for those who sought to destroy it.

... and war-time destruction

RENAMO guerrillas deliberately targeted schools and teachers, many times in horrific manner, burning classrooms, hacking teachers to death, and carrying school children into captivity. During the war, over 3,000 schools were destroyed or abandoned.

Teaching in RENAMO-held zones was rare. By all accounts, when it did exist, the quality was poor. Mostly untrained, the teachers had virtually no materials and had to rely on a few stolen textbooks (with all references to FRELIMO scribbled out) or occasional gifts from right-wing foreign missionaries.

While hundreds of rural schools stopped functioning, urban schools became — and remain — impossibly over-crowded. Classrooms burst at the seams, with 50 to 80 children crammed together, trying to learn from a single teacher. Many urban schools operate a three-shift system, with some children starting at six in the morning and others finishing school after ten at night.

Education, already devastated by the civil war, suffered still more from severe public-spending restrictions introduced under the government's economic adjustment programme in 1987. Staff morale is still very low, even though the first post-elections budget immediately slashed military spending by half and increased the education budget by over 50 per cent on the year before. But teachers still work heavy schedules and long hours in tough working conditions, for salaries

Cheia-Cheia School, Nipepe, Niassa Province: no books, no desks, just a hunger to learn
JENNY MATTHEWS/OXFAM

which have failed to keep up with inflation.

Chalk: a new-found luxury

Velosa Freitas stands at the blackboard, planning her lessons for the week. Diminished by the mountains surrounding the tiny town of Nauela, the little school of one classroom and an office boasts few materials. But Velosa holds a piece of chalk, and that is a new-found luxury.

She began teaching years ago in a local mission school, but it was abandoned when RENAMO captured the town. Velosa says, 'They never threatened to kill me, and I kept on teaching. But it was hard. We lived in the bush and taught in huts which the children had built. We had no books or chalks. All the lessons came from our heads.'

After the elections, the government decreed that all State-registered teachers from RENAMO areas could start work at government schools again. Velosa came back to town. Some of her untrained colleagues from the war years, however, are still running classes out in the bush, with no books or salaries.

The government's post-war policy to expand education is severely limited by lack of resources, at the same time as hundreds of thousands of children, unreachable before, are clamouring to learn. The problem is compounded by politics. As RENAMO desperately holds out for salaries that the government has declined to pay to its untrained teachers, its members stop government teachers working in some RENAMO strongholds.

According to the District Director of Education in Nipepe, Patricio Mutupi, after the war only one trained RENAMO teacher presented himself, while all the rest were educated only to Second or Third Grade. Fortunately, in this region they did not resist the entry of government teachers. Nipepe's main problem is lack of teaching resources.

The new school in Natili has 151 pupils aged 7 to 14. School Director Horacio Jose bemoans a shortage of books, writing materials, desks, and chairs. For sports,

the children make their own footballs, using banana leaves, but a new one has to be made for every game. Even if parents could afford school books, not a single trader in the district is selling them.

When the school re-opened in 1995, it received a gift of free books and pens for its pupils. Now, the school is trying to solve some of its own problems. Part of the donation it received was two kilos of sunflower seeds. Students learned how to sow and harvest on the school field. With profits from the 40 kilos of seeds they produced, Jose plans to buy school benches.

In 1995, the re-elected FRELIMO government decided to allow local-language teaching into schools for the first time. It pledged to rebuild the war-destroyed education network and integrate former teachers back into the system. The challenge is still enormous: in the same year, one million children of primary-school age were out of school because no places were available.

A road to nowhere?

In the far north of Mozambique, Mocimboa da Praia town is a sad relic of its former self. Before the war of independence, it boasted piped water, electric lights, an international airport where Boeing planes would land, a tennis club, seaside villas, and a buzzing import–export trade with Europe and India. These days the town is paralysed, water rarely runs through the pipes, the old warehouses are closed, and the villas stand decrepit. Reaching Mozambique's northern-most district of Palma, under a black sky heavy with rain, feels like reaching the end of Africa or the end of the last century.

While thousands of children elsewhere in Mozambique are out of school because there are no places, in Palma the position is reversed. Every year, the teachers set out on a thankless door-to-door round, trying to persuade local parents to send their children to school. At the mere sight of a teacher, local children run away.

There seem to be complex reasons why most Palma families have rejected the State education system. According to the teachers, most of the parents never went to school themselves and find it hard to see the advantage of education. While school children need fees, books, and clothes they can barely afford, out-of-school children help in the fields, growing food for the family, catch fish, or take themselves to neighbouring Tanzania to trade sea-foods in exchange for soap, salt, and oil.

Many of the Muslim Makwe, remembering colonial times, still associate school with the Christian religion, and if anything prefer their children to learn how to read and write in Koranic classes with Muslim teachers.

School in Palma goes no further than Grade Five; any child who qualifies for Grade Six must move out of the district to boarding school, sometimes hundreds of miles away. In 1994, only 12 of some 7,000 children in Palma went away to study. Few parents will take the risk or can afford the expense. The District Director of Education is almost despairing. 'The benefits of education in Palma are nil,' he says, claiming that, without schooling beyond Grade Five, most pupils are doomed to go nowhere but back to the rudimentary fishing and farming of their parents — so re-inforcing the idea that school is a waste of money and time.

A recent project to attract the children themselves into education had some success, when a gift of footballs and skipping ropes to local schools encouraged them to attend classes. However, education officials say that plans to supply textbooks and rebuild the ruined classrooms where children sit on broken floors under falling roofs will provide a greater incentive.

Taking another track, Palma craftspeople are doing their bit to develop local skills and stimulate the district economy, in the hope that eventually more trade and better jobs will give students a goal to aim at. Oliveira Iasine learned his trade as a tailor in colonial times, and for almost 20 years he worked alone. Then in 1994 he agreed to take on apprentices. He and a colleague received two machines from an aid organisation when they took on ten apprentices. One is Fatima Jameson, born and bred in Palma, who had no trade or chance of earning money until Oliveira opened his doors. With a few months' training, she makes simple clothes for children. 'One day I'd like to have my own machine, and train others,' she says.

Fatima Jameson, apprentice tailor, with her baby in the workshop of Oliveira Iasine in Palma, Cabo Delgado Province

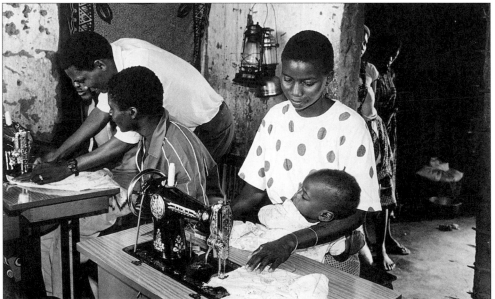

Health:
the jaded jewel

In 1991, health workers in Zambezia Province were pelted with stones when they arrived to vaccinate a terrified community against common diseases. Unused to modern health care, the people believed that the health workers had come to suck out their blood.

Despite a rapid expansion of health-care services since Independence, throughout the 1980s only about one third of the Mozambican people ever had access to modern health care. The rest depended on traditional medicine practised by herbalists and the intervention of spirits through spirit mediums. But the practice of *curandeiros* (the collective name for herbalists and traditional healers) was outlawed at national independence. They were not legally allowed to work again until 1992.

The ancient art of the curandeira

Lacaloue Mucuhota, a *curandeira* from the village of Cheia-Cheia, doesn't know when she was born, but remembers the German invasion of Mozambique (1917). Long ago, she fell very sick; once cured, she asked her saviour to teach her healing.

She treats simple illnesses with a variety of roots; but should someone fall very ill, a complex ritual is followed to restore them to full health. The patient must bring a gazelle. The animal's blood is mixed with roots and a little piece of each organ — liver, heart, lungs — and other parts of its body. All the *curandeiras* of the village are called. They cook this 'strong medicine' for the patient, then sing and dance all night outside the patient's house. Next they bring sorghum and plant it outside the house. When it is ripe, they are called back to make sorghum flour. With this, the *curandeiras* make *otogoa*, a sweet drink,

and sing and dance all night again. In the morning they bathe the patient, before painting his or her face and shoulders. Taking one or two years to complete, the ritual finally ends after bananas have been grown and eaten outside the patient's house.

Lacaloue and her group of younger *curandeiras* say the last time they performed this ceremony was before the war. Now there is much hunger in the village, and all they can do is cook the strong medicine.

The jewel in FRELIMO's crown

Statistics show that Mozambique has one of the world's least healthy populations. From a population of approximately 17 million, every year some 200,000 children die before the age of five. Some 20 per

Lacaloue Mucuhota with other traditional healers, making music in Cheia-Cheia, Niassa Province
JENNY MATTHEWS/OXFAM

53

Niassa Province:
a mother-and-baby clinic
which managed to
function during the civil
war
CHRIS JOHNSON/OXFAM

to 4,000 by 1985. FRELIMO's health-care achievements won enthusiastic praise from the World Health Organisation. They were the jewel in FRELIMO's socialist crown.

As with education, however, health care became both a symbol of FRELIMO achievement and a target for attack. During the war, some 85 per cent of health facilities were destroyed or abandoned or could not be maintained. By 1993, only 30 per cent of rural people had access to the health service. There were 435 doctors for the whole country and only one nurse for every 4,500 people.

FRELIMO gave up the dream of State-provided, free health care for all. In 1991 a new law allowed private medical practice to compete with the services of the State. The government renounced its hostility to *curandeiros* and agreed with donors on a new health policy aimed at 'cost recovery'. In other words, patients must pay, with the eventual aim of making health services fund themselves. It is sure to be a long haul. People already complain about the expense: 1,500 meticais (about 10 pence) to see a doctor and a 10,000 mt fee for hospital admission, plus the cost of tests and medicines, in the rural areas; 80,000 mt for an urgent appointment in the city. Yet current funding for health care relies overwhelmingly on donors.

Health care is once again top of the government agenda. When FRELIMO won the elections, it increased the health budget by 22 per cent and promised 64 new health centres and 11 rural and two general hospitals in the next five years.

A visit to a health post

Life is returning to the tiny rural town of Nauela, site of a major RENAMO base during the war. The town hall is still a roofless, empty shell, with grass growing inside. But demobilised soldiers are helping to level the road, a lively market is returning, and recently the local health post was fixed up again. Its walls are neatly plastered and freshly painted. The treatment room is clean as a whistle. On a little table there are scissors and a few

cent of babies are born underweight, and life expectancy at birth is only 45.5 years. The reaper's chief agents are malnutrition and diseases that can be prevented and treated when resources exist; they include malaria, diarrhoea, tuberculosis, and other acute respiratory diseases.

Under Portuguese rule, modern health care did not extend far beyond the city hospitals, where doctors attended the colonial class. FRELIMO nationalised the system, making it virtually free, built hundreds of rural health-care posts, and launched a new policy based on preventative care for the rural population. The number of health-care staff doubled other implements. There is no bench for patients to sit on, no cotton-wool or bandages.

Nurse Jose Maria sits at his desk, proud of the building, but worried about his patients. As so often, he has no medicines to treat them with. The best he can do is write a prescription and tell them to look in the District capital, some 50 km away. There is no bus. The health post has a fridge, but it doesn't work. The vaccination campaign has stopped, because Jose has no transport.

Post-war rehabilitation of the health system will not only be about buildings. It is just as much about supply and distribution of staff, equipment, and medicines. It is about making scarce resources stretch as far as possible.

Taking health care to the community

Local health authorities in Cabo Delgado are trying to re-activate a withered network of community health assistants. Roises Momade joined the community health team in 1980, when popular enthusiasm for FRELIMO's revolutionary health programme was still high. Roises recounts, 'The people of my village chose me to go for health training. Government officials explained that they could not afford to pay us, but the village population promised to support its health workers. We had six months' training and received medical kits, although local support never materialised.'

For fresh supplies, Roises was obliged to walk to the nearest government health centre, 45 km away from his home, or 11 hours' walking with no rest. Eventually in 1989 he was called for further training and received a new bicycle. Despite the lack of rewards, Roises never gave up. 'I like this work. People always come to me with their problems.' He deals mainly with malaria, coughs and colds, diarrhoea, and stomach aches. Now the health authorities in Mocimboa are looking for new means to give people like Roises some reward for their dedication and to reactivate the CHW network.

AIDS: the irony of peace

One condition that Mozambican health workers are ill-equipped to deal with is AIDS, a problem which bitter irony dictates is likely to get rapidly worse in peace time. Mozambique's war-time isolation and the paralysis of most normal migration and trade kept the country relatively immune from the AIDS virus sweeping through Southern Africa.

With the return of hundreds of thousands of refugees from AIDS-afflicted neighbouring countries, and as people and traffic flow normally back and forth across the borders again, conditions are ripe for AIDS to launch a widespread attack on Mozambique.

Access to contraceptive services is virtually nil in most rural areas, while men commonly enjoy multiple relationships. Economic hardship, combined with liberalisation, has meanwhile brought a resurgence of prostitution.

The Pemba Amateur Theatre Group, formed by five health professionals, two cultural workers, two policemen, and one prison guard, is doing what little it can to spread the warning of danger from AIDS and to advise about protection. Theatre Group director Joao Andala says, 'No one will come to hear boring speeches. We use theatre to entertain people, and teach them at the same time.'

Social action

In most places in Mozambique, health care is still expected to be a delivery system. In Cabo Delgado, however, the government's social welfare body, Accao Social (AS), is taking a fresh approach.

The first step is to identify the most vulnerable social groups, least able to provide for themselves and their families. These include people with disabilities, people with long-term illnesses, and the many single mothers struggling to raise children alone.

The next step is helping them to make the most of their meagre resources. AS volunteers are learning to work with disabled people using a new

CHRIS JOHNSON/OXFAM

methodology, the 'ABC' approach. This aims to teach disabled people, their families, and friends about care within the community. It can mean anything from teaching disabled people how to dress themselves more easily, to improving physiotherapy techniques, to making prosthetic limbs and wheel-chairs from locally available materials.

Remigio Namaunde began work as a teacher, at the age of 15, in the liberation war. But an accident left him without the use of one leg and, unfit to stand for long hours, he lost his job. Now he works for AS as a volunteer. Remigio says, 'The ABC method changes the idea that disabled people should just receive handouts. We don't give things away, but teach people to help themselves.' AS has distributed free wheel-chairs to some disabled children: but only on condition that they attend school.

Another line of 'social action' is teaching family planning and nutrition to mothers. Co-ordinator of AS in Mocimboa, Francisco Machava, says, 'Many local families eat only one meal a day, usually rice or flour with fish. We advise on varying the grain, and adding beans and vegetables to enrich the diet.' Dietary planning can help a lot, but is not enough by itself to solve the problem of poor nutrition. AS-Mocimboa is trying to help local women to find ways of raising their income.

Fading traditions

Older generations everywhere tend to complain that modern youth are losing respect for traditional values. In Mozambique, the reasons are more compelling than usual. Unlike some African countries, which celebrated their indigenous traditions after freedom from colonial rule, Mozambican culture suffered a rude blow in 1975. The Marxist new government relabelled tradition as 'superstition' and outlawed many of its practices, such as polygamy, traditional healing, and initiation rites for young men and women.

Tradition dies, but dies hard. Despite the ban, many communities continued their age-old practices, which are now legal again since the ban was lifted in 1990. In the more isolated regions of northern Mozambique, every young person must still pass through the rites of initiation, even if these have assumed a modified form. Rituals vary from region to region.

Macua

When a girl in Nipepe District, Niassa, reaches puberty, the time has come for initiation. First she is forbidden to put salt on food, and may not do so again until completing the ritual. (However, she may never in the future use salt during menstruation.) An older woman of the village will take the adolescent girls out into the bush, where they spend a week learning about adult life, respect for parents, and marital relations. At last, they bathe in the river, then paint their faces with clear, shining oil before donning a veil. The veiled girls are led to the local chief's house, who must now give a gift before lifting each veil. The proceeds are kept by the elderly teacher.

While initiation rites continue, the Macua tradition of scarring is dying out. The practice of cutting patterns into a woman's flesh, supposedly to make her more attractive, has given way to wearing beads.

Makonde

It almost seems a contradiction that the staunchly pro-FRELIMO Makonde people are among those who have best guarded their traditions. Adolescent boys are taken into the bush, where they must live apart from the village while they learn about hunting and the duties of a man and husband, such as his obligation to build a house, clear fields, and provide clothes for his wife. They also learn a mysterious dance, named after the spirit Mapiko. Traditionally the dance is performed in wooden masks and grass skirts, with rattles worn on the feet. Makonde initiation for boys includes circumcision.

Wearing their Mapiko disguise, the young men first return to their villages for a dance festival. Women and younger boys are meant to be amazed, wondering who the dancers are. The elders of Makonde territory in Mueda lament that 'Mapiko used to be a secret; people believed it was a spirit. But now the mystery has died and respect is dying with it. Boys still go through initiation, but

The clash of old and new: a Macua girl in traditional mask, Mocimboa da Praia, Cabo Delgado Province
JENNY MATTHEWS/OXFAM

they come back the same. It's not like the old days.' Even so, the old men refuse to show their Mapiko masks, carved from ebony, in front of strangers.

Gentle birth

Only a small proportion of Mozambican women ever give birth in a hospital. Most are assisted, if at all, by traditional midwives — elderly women of the village or suburb where they live. The midwives have no equipment and their techniques are often rudimentary. Hospital data show a maternal death rate of 300 per 100,000 live births, but other data suggest that nationally the figure is more like 1,000 deaths. (In England the rate is eight deaths per 100,000 live births.)

Felismena Jacinto of N'tamba, Cabo Delgado, gave birth to her eighth child, as to the others, without assistance. When she felt the pains, she went to her room alone, not calling the family until labour was over. Six of her children are living; her twins died young. The nearest maternity unit was 7 km away (much nearer than for most women).

Nearness isn't always enough. Women in Ruace District of Zambezia complain that many give birth on the doorstep of the maternity ward, because nurses refuse to help them without payment, which they can't afford.

Local women testify to gradually improving assistance in Cabo Delgado. Grandmother Caterina Tiago learned midwifery from her own grandmother, at a time when tradition allowed only *curandeiras* to learn the skill. 'My grandmother taught me what she knew,' says Caterina. 'But midwives here used to have many problems. For example, we used to cut the umbilical cord with a sharp piece of straw, but often the wound became infected. If a baby was late, we would rush to give the mother traditional medicines; if the baby was born with breathing problems, we had no other solution than putting tobacco up its nostrils to make it sneeze, or bathing it in the water from soaked maize — but this didn't always work.'

Following a new local strategy to work with existing community skills, from 1990 traditional midwives in Cabo Delgado have selectively been called in to Mocimboa for professional training. Village communities are asked to choose midwives for the training, which involves teaching principles of hygiene and sterilisation, and simple techniques such as using sterilised knives to cut the umbilical cord, wrapping the baby in a clean cloth, cleaning secretions, and giving the baby resuscitation if it has trouble in breathing. The midwives are also taught to predict difficult cases and refer them to health centres.

After her re-training, Caterina received a kit with an apron, sterilisation dishes, gloves, and other basic equipment. She says, 'It is God's will that some women here still die in labour; but since we were re-trained, the cases are now very few.'

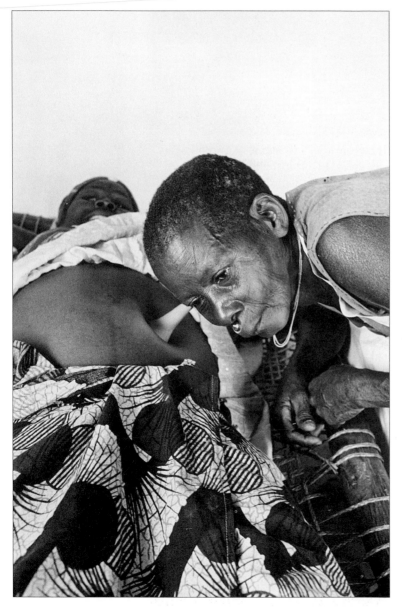

Caterina Tiago, a traditional midwife chosen by her community to receive professional training
JENNY MATTHEWS/OXFAM

A mother's right

Mozambique's long history of male labour migration, of displaced communities, wartime insecurity, and economic decline has whittled away at the traditional values which bound families together and at extended family networks, which used to offer support if marriages broke down and couples separated. From the far north to the deep south, countless thousands of Mozambican women are now forced to shoulder the entire burden of family survival, alone.

Fisherwoman and farmer from the coastal town of Mocimboa da Praia, in northern Cabo Delgado Province, Awa Adamo has given birth to 14 children, of whom nine have survived. One was struck blind by measles. One of her three husbands went to work in Tanzania and never came back; the third left her for another wife while Awa sat in hospital with their sick baby son. None has ever helped her with maintenance for the children. Awa says, 'I can't afford to send my children to a government school. I tried to put them in a Muslim school, but they gave up because I couldn't afford to buy them proper clothes.' She adds, 'I work as hard as I can, just to provide the family with food' — growing rice and cassava, and selling firewood, buns, and fried fish.

Awa's story is not unusual. On the Islamicised coast of north Mozambique, girls are often under pressure to marry young. Yet men apparently feel little obligation either to stay with their partners or to help care for their children. Most local marriages are religious and not recognised by the State, while Muslim tradition allows a man to take more than one wife and gives him the power to dissolve a marriage by his own written decree. Meantime, there is little local knowledge about family planning and very limited access to modern contraceptives.

Health and welfare authorities in Cabo Delgado say that women like Awa face enormous difficulties in coping alone. Family health suffers as they struggle to grow enough food. In Mocimboa, health staff say the main problem they encounter is malnutrition, adding that 80 per cent of the cases have 'social causes'.

Making the law work for women

Susana Carlos of Palma District, Cabo Delgado, is the local co-ordinator of MULEIDE, a Mozambican NGO concerned with Women, Law, and Development. According to Susana,

Another child registered: another success for MULEIDE
JENNY MATTHEWS/OXFAM

'After a few years of living together, a local man will often leave his family, usually taking every last thing, down to the very clothes on his wife's body.' Furthermore, 'When a husband dies, the man's family usually takes everything.'

These practices contradict modern Mozambican law, which recognises a spouse's right to alimony and inheritance and gives children the right to receive support and inherit goods from both their parents. MULEIDE argues that the problem is less with the law itself than with its application. The problem begins with ignorance. In a country where 79 per cent of women are illiterate (compared with 55 per cent of men) and where few people have any experience of the modern judicial system, single mothers are rarely aware that legal protection exists. Furthermore they have no experience of dealing with official courts, whose bureaucracy and expense are beyond their capacity to cope with.

Despite its principle of equality for women and men, the law also has loopholes, leaving thousands of mothers unprotected. Based on Portuguese colonial law, Mozambican legislation ignores the customary ceremonies and *de facto* marriages which bind the majority of couples. It recognises only marriages registered by the State and protects only children registered by the State.

Susana explains, 'MULEIDE is encouraging women to register both their marriages and their children, as this gives them a legal footing to claim maintenance if the marriage breaks up, and to inheritance, in the case of death.' Although they have not managed to register any marriages yet, 'because the men are reluctant', in eight months MULEIDE in Palma helped to register 565 children with the local authorities.

At national level, MULEIDE is setting up offices where free legal advice and counselling will be offered to women with little or no income.

MULEIDE member Mwanasa Alberto says that, in a society where men usually control the money, beyond demanding their legal rights women need new ways to increase their income and thus attain economic independence. Her organisation is running courses in basic business management.

In Mocimboa, single mother Awa Adamo has become a model entrepreneur. Recently she began growing a variety of vegetables on her little seaside plot. The work is easier than ordinary farming. Her family diet has improved and she has saved up money from vegetable sales to buy new clothes for her children.

Awa Adamo on her vegetable plot in Mocimboa da Praia, Cabo Delgado Province
JENNY MATTHEWS/OXFAM

The challenge of democracy

Mozambique emerged from civil war proclaiming its will to weave a newly democratic nation from the shreds of its old social fabric. It had few threads to weave with. There is no tradition of civic organisations independent of the ruling hierarchies.

At village level, the rules of traditional society have changed little in the last 500 years. Rural chiefs still allocate land, mete out local justice, and communicate with divine powers through the mediation of their own ancestral spirits. Order is pre-ordained through blood, as the chief passes power down to his sons.

On a national plane, State powers were heavily centralised. Portuguese colonials suppressed the emergence of independent African organisations, banning trade unions, and viewing membership of other African groups and the many independent churches as 'political' and subversive.

At Independence from Portugal, FRELIMO sought to control not only political and economic life, but also civil society. It banned all opposition groups and created 'organisations of the masses', intended to represent the interests of various social groups and to propagate party ideology. Thus the Mozambican Workers' Organisation (OTM) was charged with mobilising workers to meet production targets set by the government's central economic plan. The Mozambican Women's Organisation (OMM) and Mozambique Youth Organisation (OJM) were meant to identify the needs of women and young people, and teach them FRELIMO's ideology. In the countryside, FRELIMO organised villagers into collective co-operatives. For many Mozambicans, co-operative organisation still bears the stigma of the failed collectives. Under Mozambique's first national constitution, there was no legal space to create independent, civic organisations.

The result was a gulf between the organised institutions of the party/State and ordinary groups of citizens, who lacked an independent voice to express their local and particular interests. Eventually FRELIMO admitted that it had been a mistake to exclude all independent voices from the public arena, and that its attempt at comprehensive social engineering had ultimately failed. Meanwhile, the burden of national debt, widespread poverty, and strong pressure from foreign donors and creditors made it impossible to carry on the experiment.

Separating State, judicial, and political powers, the new constitution adopted in 1990 enshrines the rights to freedom of thought, religion, expression, information, and association. Any group of citizens may now form an independent association.

To some, it was a double-edged gift. The 'organisations of the masses' were suddenly told to fend for themselves: they must become politically and financially independent. In line with the trend to liberal isation, foreign donors have gradually redirected much of their support away from State institutions towards independent and private organisations. While on the one hand the pressure to channel funds through NGOs has further weakened the State, on the other hand it has led international NGOs to promote the creation of national ones. Sceptics say that many of the newly emerging national NGOs are donor-inspired and donor-driven.

Others argue that a novel space has been created in which civil society is finally able to evolve. Mozambicans have a tough but historic opportunity to rebuild their society from the ashes of the old.

Mozambique: Facts and figures

Area: 779,380 sq km (UK 243,360 sq km)

Population: 17 million (1995)

Population growth rate: 4.9 per cent (1995)

Growth rate of Gross Domestic Product: 4.5 per cent (1995)

Life expectancy: 45.5 (1995)

Under-five mortality rate: 282 deaths per 1,000 live births (1993) (UK: 8 per 1,000)

Number of doctors: 381; 1 per 40,900 inhabitants (1993)

Number of nurses: 3,690; 1 per 4,223 per inhabitants

CARMOC cardboard box factory in Maputo
JENNY MATTHEWS/OXFAM

Languages: Portuguese (official) and three main African language groups: Tsonga, Sena-Nyanja, Makua-Lomwe

Literacy: Male 45 per cent, female 21 per cent (1990)

Religions: Some 300 registered religious confessions, including Muslim (c.4 million followers) and Christian (3 million Catholics, 3 million Protestants). Traditional faiths are widespread and often combined with belief in another faith.

Currency: metical
Average exchange rate in 1992: US$1.00 = 2,432 mt
Exchange rate in January 1996: US$1.00 = 9,900 mt

GDP shares: Commerce and services 33.4 per cent; agriculture 26.5 per cent; transport and communications 14.4 per cent; industries and fishing 15.1 per cent; construction 10.6 per cent (1994)

Annual export earnings: US$165 million (1995)

Annual imports: US$1,090 million (1995)

Gross Domestic Product per capita: US$88 (1994)

Foreign debt: US$5.4 billion (1994)

Main exports: prawns, cashew, cotton, sugar, copra, wood, and minerals

Main imports: consumer goods, equipment and spare parts, oil

Sources
Country Reports, Economic Intelligence Unit
The State of the World's Children, 1995, UNICEF
Public Information Bureau, The Government of Mozambique

Further reading and sources

Mozambique: the Troubled Transition by Hans Abrahamson and Anders Nilsson (Zed Books, London, 1995)

Conspicuous Destruction: War, Famine and the Reform Process in Mozambique, report by Africa Watch (Human Rights Watch, USA, 1992)

Landmines in Mozambique, The Arms Project, Africa Watch (Human Rights Watch, USA, 1994)

Frontline Nationalism in Angola and Mozambique by David Birmingham (James Currey, London, 1992)

Mozambique: Country Profile/Reports, profile and quarterly reports (Economic Intelligence Unit, London)

A Complicated War: The Harrowing of Mozambique by William Finnegan (University of California Press, 1992)

Mozambique: Who Calls the Shots? by Joseph Hanlon (James Currey, London, 1991)

Mozambique: Elections and Freedom of Expression, by Gil Lauriciano (Article 19, International Centre Against Censorship, London, 1994)

Mozambique Inview, bi-monthly review; ed: Gil Lauriciano (Mediacoop, Maputo)

Apartheid's Contras: An Inquiry into the Roots of War in Angola and Mozambique by William Minter (Zed Books, London, 1994)

A History of Mozambique by Malyn Newitt (Hurst and Company, London 1995)

Renamo: From Terrorism to Democracy in Mozambique? by Alex Vines (James Currey, London, 1995)

Angola and Mozambique: The Aftermath of Conflict by Alex Vines (Research Institute for the Study of Conflict and Terrorism, 1995)

Sources

Mozambique (Country Kit) by Ruth Ansah Ayisi (UNICEF, Maputo 1995)

Mozambique Peace Process Bulletin, Joseph Hanlon, Rachel Waterhouse, Gil Lauriciano (Association of European Parliamentarians for Africa (AWEPA)

Beggar Your Neighbours by Joseph Hanlon (CIIR/James Currey, London, 1986)

Mozambique: from Colonialism to Revolution, by Allen and Barbara Isaacman (Zimbabwe Publishing House, Harare, 1983)

'Who We Are: Voices from Mozambique' by Lorraine Johnson (1995, unpublished)

Numbers — Mozambique, Public Information Office, Maputo, 1994

Historia de Mocambique: primeiras sociedades sedentarias e impacto dos mercadores (200/300 — 1886), collective publication of the History Department, Eduardo Mondlane University (UEM, Maputo, 1988)

Mocambique: Perspectivas Economicas, edited by Carlos Nuno Castel-Branco (University of Eduardo Mondlane, Maputo 1994)

Schoolboy in Palma Primary School, Cabo Delgado Province
JENNY MATTHEWS/OXFAM

Oxfam in Mozambique

Oxfam (UK and Ireland) has worked in Mozambique since 1984, mainly on emergency-relief projects in the provinces of Zambezia and Niassa, which were very severely affected by the civil war; and on rural community-development projects in Cabo Delgado, which was relatively unaffected. Most of the projects described in this book are situated in these three provinces.

From relief to development

After running large, logistically complex relief programmes in wartime, Oxfam's mostly Mozambican staff have had to adapt quickly to reconciliation and reconstruction work, such as working with Government and RENAMO authorities to rebuild roads and bridges (alongside specialist de-mining agencies); providing medical services at a demobilisation camp; and supplying seeds and tools to returning refugees.

Recognising that a sustainable peace depends on the protection of people's basic rights and freedoms, Oxfam supported a project to monitor freedom of expression and press coverage during the election campaigns. Electoral education work was also supported, and Oxfam staff members participated as observers of the elections.

In the medium term, Oxfam plans to continue work on infrastructural rehabilitation projects (roads and bridges in Niassa, schools and health posts in Zambezia). In the longer term, the Niassa programme will focus on Food Security Development: helping local people to grow a wider range of crops, process their produce, get better access to markets, and start up micro-enterprises such as carpentry and tin-smithing with small loans. In Zambezia (which has a more resilient local economy), the long-term focus will be on supporting disabled people: helping those injured by landmines to travel to prosthesis clinics, to be fitted with artificial limbs which will give them physical independence, and supporting them with small grants to establish micro-enterprises.

Advocacy work

One in every 2,000 people in Mozambique is the victim of a landmine. Oxfam supports representatives of the disabled in their campaign for a national and international ban on the sale, production, and use of landmines. Oxfam funds them to attend conferences, to host visits by international delegations and journalists, and to organise radio broadcasts, concerts, and exhibitions.

This kind of advocacy work is an important component of Oxfam's work in Mozambique. The team also conducts and supports work which aims to address the root causes of the country's poverty: researching the details of Mozambique's enormous external debts; informing representatives of the World Bank and foreign creditor governments about the impact of Structural Adjustment policies on poor people; and promoting debate in the media about alternative strategies. Oxfam has helped to establish a lobbying/research forum, consisting of Mozambican academics, economists, and trade unionists, and representatives of the churches and of international and national voluntary agencies, to pursue these issues and seek to influence the policies of the appropriate institutions.